feng shui

Made Easy

❖ Also in the Made Easy series ❖

feng shui

Made Easy

create health, wealth and happiness through the power of your home

davina mackail

HAY HOUSE

Carlsbad, California • New York City
London • Sydney • New Delhi

Published in the United Kingdom by:
Hay House UK Ltd, Astley House, 33 Notting Hill Gate, London W11 3JQ
Tel: +44 (0)20 3675 2450; Fax: +44 (0)20 3675 2451; www.hayhouse.co.uk

Published in the United States of America by:
Hay House Inc., PO Box 5100, Carlsbad, CA 92018-5100
Tel: (1) 760 431 7695 or (800) 654 5126
Fax: (1) 760 431 6948 or (800) 650 5115; www.hayhouse.com

Published in Australia by:
Hay House Australia Ltd, 18/36 Ralph St, Alexandria NSW 2015
Tel: (61) 2 9669 4299; Fax: (61) 2 9669 4144; www.hayhouse.com.au

Published In India by:
Hay House Publishers India, Muskaan Complex, Plot No.3, B-2,
Vasant Kunj, New Delhi 110 070
Tel: (91) 11 4176 1620; Fax: (91) 11 4176 1630; www.hayhouse.co.in

Text © Davina MacKail, 2016

The moral rights of the author have been asserted.

The information given in this book should not be treated as a substitute for professional medical advice; always consult a medical practitioner. Any use of information in this book is at the reader's discretion and risk. Neither the author nor the publisher can be held responsible for any loss, claim or damage arising out of the use, or misuse, of the suggestions made, the failure to take medical advice or for any material on third-party websites.

This book was previously published under the title *Feng Shui* (*Hay House Basics* series); ISBN: 978-1-78180-629-6

A catalogue record for this book is available from the British Library.

ISBN: 978-1-78817-257-8

To everyone with a home, however humble, may your Land Spirits always be truly blessed.

Contents

List of Exercises

Acknowledgements

Without all the people who have invited me into their houses over the last 20 years this book could not have come into being. I am truly grateful for all that you and your homes have taught me.

Deep gratitude also goes to Gina Lazenby for her courage and vision in promoting feng shui, and all my many feng shui teachers, too numerous to mention individually by name, you know who you are. I honour, acknowledge and am grateful for all you have taught me and all of your dedication to this work, helping people awaken to the power of their homes.

With deep gratitude and heartfelt thanks to the endless loving support of Nizami Cummins, Carla Miles and my dearest Mum – without you this journey would be a great deal harder and far less fun.

Thank you to all the wonderful team at Hay House and, in particular, Amy Kiberd, Julie Oughton and Sandy Draper, who have worked tirelessly to ensure this book gets to print in a timely manner.

And last, but not least, thank you to my new home and its fascinating and complex feng shui, which has helped shape this book in myriad ways as it reveals to me further feng shui subtleties.

> *When there is light in the soul, there*
> *is beauty in the person;*
> *When there is beauty in the person,*
> *there is harmony in the home;*
> *When there is harmony in the home;*
> *there is honour in the nation;*
> *When there is honour in the nation;*
> *there is peace in the world.*
> OLD CHINESE PROVERB

Introduction

'There's no place like home.'
DOROTHY, *THE WIZARD OF OZ*

In its fullest expression feng shui is a complex, multidisciplined and multilayered subject. Its practice is a broad umbrella covering cosmology, astrology, clutter and space clearing, interior design and placement, colour, five elements theory, yin and yang, geomancy and the in-depth study of the *IChing* – the ancient Chinese *Book of Changes*. What is written is often misleading and confusing with several schools and approaches peppered with different theories and ideas.

Yet feng shui is really quite simple to use, governed by fundamental principles that, once you understand them, like Ariadne's golden thread, can lead you safely through the maze of confusion to the ultimate goal – harmony in your home and life.

We're going to strip the subject down to its core principles, demystifying and debunking the myths, to shine a light on its practical applications and how they work in a modern context. Armed with this knowledge anyone can practise feng shui in a safe, common-sense way and use it to bring great benefit to their life and the lives of those they share space with.

I encourage you to seek out other books and teachers and explore the topic widely. Feng shui is a body of philosophical thought and therefore its solutions are open to interpretation, depending on the training and subjective synthesis of the practitioner. Just as you could ask many architects or designers for their opinion on your home, and each would give you a different and equally valid answer, it's a mistake to believe there is only one way or a 'right' way to do feng shui. There can be many answers to the same problem.

My feng shui journey

I'm deeply passionate about feng shui and its power to transform. My life is entirely unrecognizable from when I discovered it 20 years ago. In fact it feels more like a past life rather than a former aspect of this one! Back then I was a consultant for a premium-rate telecoms company, travelling the world, setting up chat lines and other services. It became intolerable when I was flown home to manage a live, chat-line company to fill the shoes of a former manager who had been fired for fraud.

Commuting weekly to Leeds from Cambridge, my clean driving licence was wiped out with speeding tickets in six months, such was my haste to escape the place each day. I had a panic button on my desk with a direct link to the local police station and the local officers were frequent visitors, as there always seemed to be some kind of 'trouble'. My office window looked out on a bleak piece of tarmac surrounded by barbed-wire fencing. I was utterly miserable: away from home, isolated, unsupported and unable to do the job assigned to me due to the antagonism of the staff, who saw me as the outsider, not to be trusted and 'different' from them. None of it was working and I didn't know what to do.

As the saying goes, 'When the student is ready, the teacher appears' – I was definitely ready. One day I came across an article that mentioned feng shui and that eventually led me to the UK's only school of feng shui at that time, the Feng Shui Network International, founded by Gina Lazenby. Gina captured the zeitgeist of the moment. Her magnificent PR efforts ensured that many people now know about feng shui, having used it or heard about its benefits. I was extraordinarily blessed to be one of the school's first students. Gina worked hard to find international experts capable of teaching us.

I first heard of feng shui when I was in China, working in Hong Kong in the telecoms industry, and there was very little information about the subject available in English. However, I was a long-time student of the *I Ching* (which translates as *The Book of Changes* – an ancient Chinese oracle), and when I started delving into the subject, it helped me make sense of so much I had already read. I am eternally grateful for my feng shui journey and the miracles of manifestation it has created, and continues to create, each and every day. My awareness of feng shui is still evolving and for me it is primarily about *chi* (energy) flow, the Spirit of Place and environmental psychology.

Why feng shui?

Our homes are the most intimate external expression of who we are. As the English designer and one of the pioneers of the Arts & Crafts Movement, William Morris, said, 'Home is metaphor of the Self.' When we dream of houses at night, they are symbolic of the 'mansion of our soul' – understanding our home is a master key to understanding who we are. Feng shui helps us to understand ourselves through our external reflection. We all unconsciously and intuitively place artworks and personal items around our homes, in order to represent what's going on inside us. The layout of each room, the position of the furniture, the flow of foot traffic, where we spend most time, the storage of items, the organizing of equipment, the total design of the living space all speak volumes about the people we are and how we feel about ourselves and each other. Feng shui allows us to 'see' ourselves through the eyes of our home and choose to change. It has often been called the 'art of placement' in the West.

It is not a magical, miracle cure but good feng shui can help us combat the difficult times and reap the benefits from the good ones. It connects us deeply to ourselves and will allow you to know who you are, what you want and where you are going in life. It will create a new relationship with your living space: connecting you to the magic of your home – a situation where it feels like your home is giving you a loving hug hello when you walk in.

The relationships we have with our homes are the most important of all because they can help us to understand, improve and develop all the other relationships in our lives

– with our lovers, our spouses, our families and friends but, most importantly of all, with ourselves. Houses are not just piles of inanimate bricks and mortar, they are also living, breathing entities that can be enlisted in helping us attract more of what we want in life and less of what we don't want.

If you ask someone why they chose a certain house mostly they'll reply, 'Oh I walked in and immediately knew it was the house for me – it just FELT right.' This feeling is the Spirit of Place. The majority of us live somewhere, even if just a room, and the principles of feng shui apply equally to the smallest room and the grandest mansion.

I often get asked 'How do I know if my home has bad feng shui?' You know something is wrong, if you suffer a run of 'bad luck' shortly after moving into a new home or after having lived happily in a space for a number of years, life suddenly starts going wrong. If you or your family continually get sick, you suddenly get made redundant or get the sack for no apparent reason, maybe someone in the family has an accident or you get burgled, for example. Sometimes this run of bad luck can be related to your personal astrology but if all the family seem to be suffering simultaneously it's definitely worth checking your feng shui.

In our fast-changing technological world feng shui reminds us to slow down and reconnect with our living spaces and our lives. We are human 'beings' not 'doings'. We were not designed to cope with this new age of machines driving us to achieve more and more, faster and faster. We can reconnect to stillness and sacredness through cultivating our relationship with our homes.

We are going to explore the psychology of our homes as a tool for transformation. This will be a journey of self-discovery as reflected by our living spaces. Every house in the country can be 'read' if you know what to look for. I encourage you to become your own private detective searching for the clues to your archetypes and metaphors. Armed with this knowledge, you can make design and decor alterations that can range from the subtle to the dramatic in order to improve your current life situation and make your house a home.

Think it's hocus pocus? Well, there's one way to find out and that's to do it! I know feng shui attracts more than its fair share of sceptics and this is my challenge to you: make a commitment to test it for yourself. Follow the advice given, make a few changes and see what happens. Yes, you could continue to call the magic that will inevitably unfold coincidence, but I believe you will also continue the feng shui journey, as a deeper part of you will sense there's something in it, even though you can't quite put your finger on what.

Part I

GETTING STARTED

'Meet it, and you do not see
its beginning. Follow it, and
you do not see its end. Stay
with the ancient Way in order
to master what is present.'

LAO TZU

Chapter 1

How Feng Shui Works and Where It Comes From

'The Tao that can be named is not the Tao.'
LAO TSE

Feng shui evolved from the basic realization that we are affected by our surroundings and have an innate understanding of how our environments affect us. We immediately get a good feeling when we enter some houses and a bad feeling when we enter others. We know instinctively if an argument has taken place. Our language supports our understanding, hence the common expressions, 'You could cut the atmosphere with a knife' or 'That place had really bad vibes'. The ancient Chinese had a whole area of study devoted to this subject known as feng shui. Pronounced, 'fung shway' or, as I prefer, 'fun and play' because this is the best approach – to have fun and play with it. It's good to put a bit of feng shui in your life but don't put your life in feng shui!

Feng shui is a system for creating balance and harmony in our lives through the cultivation of the chi or energy flow around our homes. It is also about connecting us to the Spirit of Place we call home.

It allows us to move with the tides of life rather than against them. It teaches us how to transform and harmonize our environments to achieve more of what we want in life by harnessing the beneficial energies; and at the same time reducing what we don't want by limiting or transmuting the harmful or stagnant energies. It is a wonderful way for us to become more conscious of our co-creative abilities, empowering us to take full responsibility for our lives.

Moreover it is a powerful tool in helping us to master one of our greatest fears – the fear of change. Feng shui teaches us that nothing stays the same. The state of impermanence is the only truth. Within this state of change, we are working with the totality of parts to create a constantly mutating, holistic harmony in our homes and lives.

It's all about the chi: How feng shui works

Feng shui is based on the same principles as quantum physics: everything in the universe is connected and made of energy at the subatomic level. If two photons fly off in different directions at the speed of light and something is done to one of them, the other immediately reacts. Yet nothing can move faster than the speed of light. Between Einstein's Theory of Relativity and developments in Quantum Theory, science has begun to prove and accept what mystics and philosophers have been saying for thousands of years: that everything in the world is energetically connected.

Therefore, everything in our homes has a corresponding impact on our lives either positive or negative because we are energetically connected with them.

It is relatively easy to see how colour in a room or natural light, the style of furniture, type of art, ornaments, living plants and so on can affect our experience of a place, and determine whether or not we feel comfortable. What perhaps is more difficult to grasp immediately is the notion that invisible energy flows around us all the time and anything that affects that flow will also affect our lives. We cannot see or understand electricity, yet we don't question its effectiveness in providing light and power when we need it. This is a good attitude to adopt with feng shui. You may not be able to see the chi energy but you will certainly feel the effects of it. Similarly, we cannot see the wind but we become aware of its presence when we hear the leaves rustling. When the winds are benevolent they can help us navigate from shore to shore and when the winds are angry we're left in no doubt of their destructive power.

Exercise: Experiencing chi

Pause for a moment and rub your hands together vigorously several times. Now bring your facing palms close together but not touching. You should be able to feel a ball of invisible energy between them. An indefinable but definitely tangible sensation – that's *chi* (pronounced, *chee*) in China. If you can't feel it, rub your hands together longer and harder, and try again.

We don't have an exact word for this invisible energy known as chi or *qi*, in English. Probably the closest is life force or vital energy. Certainly many cultures are aware of its existence. It is known in India as *prana*, in Japan as *ki* and in Egypt as *ankh*. Whatever we call it, it is that vital force or energy that permeates all things: feng meaning wind and shui meaning water because the breath of chi carries both. In the Q'ero shamanic tradition, in which I'm also trained, it is referred to as the 'animating essence'. Getting to know chi – identifying it, understanding how it moves, how to harmonize it, transform it and direct it – is what feng shui is all about. In essence it is the philosophy of the cosmic dance between heaven and earth.

Trinity of luck

The ancient Chinese considered there were three types of luck or chi that affect us for better or worse:

1. Heaven luck (heaven chi)

2. Human luck (human chi)

3. Earth luck (earth chi)

Each of the trinity are considered to be a different form or type of chi, so it is worth understanding how each can affect us.

Heaven luck (chi)

This chi is fixed by the heavens on the day you were born. Some might call it fate or destiny. It comes from the sun, moon, stars and other celestial beings. This chi cannot be controlled, although it can be cultivated and it is wise to have an idea where you are in relation to the bigger schemes of things. Keeping up to date with your astrological influences, knowing your natal chart, knowing the moon times, when Mercury is retrograde and so on, can all help you stay in flow with these larger cosmic energies, enabling you to make the best of opportunities when they present themselves and know when to retreat and consolidate for best effect. Heaven chi deals with time. Your personal birth date and the birth date of your home are vital pieces of feng shui information and some form of astrology is a key component to any consultation.

Human luck (chi)

This chi is the unique signature given to us at birth. Your upbringing, life experiences, conditioning, habits, beliefs, lifestyle and work ethic all affect your human chi – it is the realm of karma. It is possible to influence this luck by personal development, cultivating awareness, a healthy lifestyle, serving the greater good and daily practice. I call this luck 'inner feng shui', which, through the practice of feng shui, happens automatically as the internal and external are connected.

Earth luck (chi)

This is the environmental chi of where we live. The mountains, trees, rivers and other buildings each hold a particular chi, as do environmental issues such as electromagnetic frequencies, power stations, underground waterways, railways and roads, pollution, noise and the objects around us – all have a chi that impacts our lives for good or bad. This is the luck chi that we can enhance using feng shui. By harnessing the earth luck, we create a bridge to heaven luck improving the flow of healthy energies in our lives. This in turn leads to better relationships, greater opportunities, increased energy and greater prosperity.

The properties of chi

Chi has certain properties that you'll come to recognize and understand with practice but are best summarized as follows:

- It is in permanent motion from one form to another.

- It accumulates, condenses, expands and disperses.

- It can be strong and weak, beneficial and harmful.

- It tends to move forwards – never leaving a space by the same route it entered – so will stagnate in cupboards or rooms with only one door and no windows, i.e. cellars.

- It can move slowly or quickly.

- It can stagnate or spiral.

- It moves up and down and in and out.

- It can rush and also meander.

- It permeates all things.

- It is the lifeblood of the universe.

Balancing sheng chi and sha chi

There are two primary conditions of chi that we can seek to balance by practising feng shui.

1. *Sheng chi*: Beneficial, healthy chi that spirals freely around a clear, clean space and is able to nourish and feed the occupants as it saunters through.

2. *Sha chi*: Harmful chi that stagnates in damp, dark corners; accumulates in blocked passageways; attacks us from overpowering furniture, buildings, other land forms, etc.; pollutes our senses through toxic smells, noise, clutter, etc.

By practicing feng shui we can cultivate sheng chi with:

- clutter-free, clean environments
- blooming, vibrant gardens
- fresh flowers and healthy plants
- pleasing artwork and decor
- beautiful music
- dancing
- birdsong
- incense
- scented candles
- soft textures
- vibrant foods
- clean water
- positive vibes, good feelings, etc.

We can also redirect or harmonize sha chi that accumulates and stagnates in:

- damp, rotting food
- chronic clutter
- overflowing rubbish bins
- dead or dying things
- weeds
- mildew, mould or damp
- broken items
- toxic fumes and pollution
- negative earth energies: black streams, geopathic stress, etc.
- sewage
- landfill sites
- violence, screaming, fights
- busy roads and intersections
- power stations, pylons, etc.
- railway cuttings and crossings
- loud noises
- flight paths
- bad vibes, toxic thought patterns, sick feelings, etc.

Exercise: Chi visualization

Sit and close your eyes for a moment. Imagine being on top of a mountain, freezing cold, in the middle of a torrential storm. How does it feel to be buffeted around in such an exposed space? It's not very comfortable is it?

Now close your eyes again and imagine lying on a tropical island, feeling the warm sun on your skin and pure white sand beneath your toes, as you listen to the gentle ebb and flow of the waves. How does that make you feel? More relaxed, happier?

This simple visualization can help you become aware of how chi in different forms will affect you very differently.

Chi affects us all, all of the time, in myriad ways, and your home is alive with chi. It may not be quite as alert as you and I but it is a living, breathing space nonetheless. I regularly 'chat' to my home and encourage you to do the same. After all 'walls have ears' – remember! I stroke the walls and thank the space for looking after me, I enjoy the act of caretaking whatever space I am living in, constantly nurturing the sheng chi and dispersing any lingering sha chi, getting to know the Spirit of Place and recognizing myself in its varying reflections. It is also a way of honouring myself by looking after the container that offers me sanctuary from the elements. Think of your home as a living spirit, care for it and it will care for you by making you feel supported and nourished.

> '(It) rides the wind and scatters, but is retained when
> encountering water.'
> STEPHEN L. FIELD, *THE ZANGSHU*

The origins of feng shui

Much of the information about feng shui comes from China. Historical data varies as to its exact age but it is in the region of 2–5,000 years old, with written records dating back at least 2,700 years. The Chinese have always believed in the 'oneness' of things and so feng shui was born out of their deep understanding of the Tao (which translates as 'The Way'), the intangible, unknowable source of all reality. Originally feng shui was called *kan yu* meaning the understanding of heaven and earth. The ancient Chinese scholars were aware of our place in the cosmic hierarchy and created formulas and practices to increase the human and earth luck factors.

Initially only emperors had access to this knowledge, using it to maintain their wealth and power, but gradually the wisdom disseminated throughout the general populace. Feng shui remains practical and relevant for our lives today and its principles are universal. Every culture, whatever they may call it, has an understanding of how humans interact with their environment: in India it is called *vastu shastra* while in Europe it's known as geomancy, for example.

Different methods

The biggest obstacle when starting your feng shui journey is discovering that different books give seemingly conflicting advice and different remedies. Without understanding why, this can be disheartening and cause you to give up before you've reaped the benefits of this wondrous practice. The reason for the confusion is that there are a number of different methods (often called schools) and approaches that will produce different results in certain circumstances. The two predominant approaches to feng shui are classical and modern. But within each of these approaches, there are a number of further subsets or schools.

Before we move on to the juicy stuff, we need to take a mini tour through feng shui's long, history to establish the different practices and methods. If it feels too early for a history lesson, or you already know it, then feel free simply to read the checklist (*see page 26*) and proceed to Chapter 2.

Traditional or classical feng shui

Exploring the history of feng shui's evolution helps us demystify the topic, as the various methods evolved to deal with particular landscapes. If we keep in mind that feng shui is predominantly about the harnessing and transforming of earth luck then we can more easily understand how and why the different methods grew into being.

> *'If one lives in a house without land spirit, everything will go wrong. His own soul will not be comforted, his career will decline and as a result misfortune will fall on him.'*
> MASTER SHENG-YEN LU

Form School

Southern China is characterized by large mountain ranges and undulating terrain, hence 'Form School', also known as landscape or 'armchair' feng shui, emerged here. Dating back to the Han dynasty (206BCE to AD220), this is the oldest documented form of feng shui and focuses primarily on the topography and orientation of the landscape, the flow of chi and balance of yin and yang energies. Feng shui masters explored the 'forms' of the land and used them to their advantage. For example, in Southern China it wouldn't be prosperous to site your farm in a valley (too damp) or facing a mountain (too dark). The ideal feng shui placement is as though you were sitting in a metaphoric armchair or, as the Chinese would say, resting in 'the belly of the dragon'. This dragon has four protective animal guardians:

- a solid mountain (turtle) behind you;
- an open view in front (phoenix), with direct access to the main source of chi, the sun;
- and protection from the destructive winds at the sides (dragon and tiger).

Using these principles, they ensured their farms produced better harvests and so more wealth and health. This approach is still relevant today, particularly in terms of siting new properties or choosing a new home, which we'll explore fully in Chapter 10.

Modern approaches to Form School may also involve analysing neighbouring buildings, walls and fences as well as natural features such as trees, hills, rivers, lakes and mountains. There is also a more specialized, some say more original, version of Form School, *Sang He feng shui*, dealing specifically with where water enters and leaves a property in order to determine the beneficial or harmful flow of chi. Although not practised widely in the West, all feng shui practitioners need to have an understanding of the importance of water chi when analysing a property.

Compass School

Northern China is flat so the topological approach of Form School didn't work. Instead Compass School evolved, which computes the feng shui of both time (heaven chi) and space (earth chi). This approach uses calculations based on a building's facing direction, determined using a compass or a Chinese *luo pan*. As with Form School, the main source of chi is the sun, as the original use of this approach was to site auspicious burial places for family vaults and, later, palaces and temples. Over time, different northern regions developed various branches of the Compass School. These use astrological formulae to calculate a person's most auspicious direction. Each method uses different data or formula for its calculations, further confusing the beginner.

Once the compass directions are established a grid called variously a *pa kua* or *bagua* or *lo shu* – all effectively the same thing and you'll learn more about them in Chapter 3 – is placed over the building and aligned to the compass directions to assign an area of the floor plan to a specific area of life. The eight life aspirations we associate with feng shui today (described in Chapter 3) are different from those considered by classical feng shui masters, who assessed the different chi flows according to predictable patterns they had observed over time, rather than believing the area had a specific function, such as health or wealth. The latter is a modern interpretation brought into being by Black Hat Sect feng shui, which we'll get to shortly.

Different branches of the Compass School include the Xuan Kong School, or Flying Stars, which works with the precise birth date of a property, and is considered by many in the East to be the highest form of feng shui, and the Ba Zhai – known as the Eight Mansions, Eight Houses or East-West School – which is highly favoured in the East.

Although these classical forms of feng shui are practised today in the West their popularity is strongest in the East where the concept of a holistic approach to life is culturally ingrained. The Western mind-set is more drawn to the environmental psychology and quick fixes of feng shui's more modern interpretations.

Contemporary feng shui

Interestingly feng shui became popular in the West in the 1960s, the same time as the Cultural Revolution in China banned its practice – although it has regained momentum in China in recent years. Modern feng shui methods are focused on what I call 'environmental psychology': the layout, decor, arrangement of furnishings and the symbolism of ornaments and artworks, to maximize the flow of chi within the space. Contemporary approaches are less concerned with complex calculations and compass directions, and most methods use the bagua aligned to the front door, rather than the magnetic compass direction, in their analyses.

Black Hat Sect, Intuitive and Three Door Gate

Professor Thomas Lin Yun brought the last formally recognized school of feng shui to the USA in the 1980s. This school is referred to as Black Sect Tantric Buddhist Feng Shui or Black Hat Sect or sometimes simply Black Hat or Black Sect. Despite its title anyone of any faith can practise its methods. This school incorporates all the teachings from both Form and Compass Schools but eliminates the use of compass directions, preferring instead to align the bagua using the front entrance of a property as the 'mouth of chi'. It was this school that assigned the eight aspirations or life areas to the bagua map. They also use what some consider quite esoteric or superstitious feng shui practices, which gave rise to feng shui 'cures', such as crystals, Chinese coins and red ribbons.

With the explosion of interest in feng shui, you might encounter a number of other Western schools, including Western Feng Shui, Pyramid Feng Shui, Intuitive Feng Shui, Instinctive Feng Shui, Three Door Gate, Fusion Feng Shui and Aspirational Feng Shui. All of these schools are evolving hybrids of traditional and modern approaches. See how confusing it gets!

How to navigate the methods for best results

Ultimately, each of these schools, whatever their individual approach, evolved their techniques to address the same fundamental issues: the importance of living in harmony with nature and assessing the chi flow within a space to maximize the flow of beneficial chi – for health, wealth and happiness – and minimize the impact of harmful chi.

All the schools have advocates who insist that their method is the one true feng shui teaching. I have been trained in both the classical and modern approaches and, as with many living teachings, my method is a hybrid version of what I learned, what I brought with me in terms of my medical and astrological background, and my ongoing shamanic practice. In other words, I inevitably practise feng shui through my subjective synthesis.

We also need to take into account that housing issues in the West differ from those in China and require a different approach. Classical feng shui was used to site buildings before they were built. Western feng shui deals predominantly with harmonizing existing structures that traditional feng shui masters would probably never have considered suitable as dwelling places in the first place!

For me the proof is in the results. Many modern-day feng shui practitioners, like myself, have healthy, prosperous businesses and profoundly enjoy assisting others to maximize their life potential. If the approach didn't work I wouldn't still be in business after 20 years. Feng shui is so encompassing and flexible that it gives rise to many possibilities for solving manifold issues, as every situation is different. I encourage you to embrace this diversity and if one method doesn't work, find another.

The primary difference between the modern and traditional approaches is in how the bagua is overlaid on a floor plan. Compass School advocates use of the geographical compass directions to align the bagua grid, whereas the modern approaches align the bagua using the front door as the main chi entrance. This latter approach is more applicable to the Western world and urban living. Our main source of chi, if living in a terrace, semi-detached house or flat, is not the sun but the front door. It is through this mouth of chi that opportunities come in the form of visitors and the daily post.

The advantage of using Compass School is the layout holds what's called an 'energy of place' that the Intuitive or Three Door Gate does not consider. For example, the physical north of a property tends to suit the colder, darker, mysterious element of water and the first house symbolism whereas the physical south of a property has the benefit of the fiery sunshine enhancing the fire element and the energies of the ninth house, etc. However, unless you are living in a detached property with land that receives 360 degrees of sunlight, these benefits are hard to realize and are therefore minimal.

Feng shui key

When laying the bagua choose one school at a time and stick to it.

Feng shui predominantly teaches us how to manage the continuous changing nature of life. As such surely it also has to be flexible and adapt with the times? We can see this is true of its history so far. Form School gave birth to Compass School, which gave birth to the Flying Stars and the Ba Zi, and so on – all different approaches, yet all ultimately involved with the intimate and intricate weaving of the ever-changing chi. For me, feng shui is a living teaching and evolves as we evolve. It cannot stay the same, rigidly attached to old tenets that no longer work with the changing times. That would be like continuing to insist on handwriting every piece of correspondence in the age of emails.

Ultimately, the approach you choose is down to which you feel most called to, what produces results and is the most applicable to your home. We're deeply conditioned to accept things in life and rarely question authority but one of the hidden benefits of feng shui is how, through its practice, we learn to question constantly and check in with ourselves about whether something 'feels' right to us or not. It teaches us to trust our inner wisdom.

All properties benefit from an assessment of their geographical layout, as taught by Form School, and this assessment won't interfere, or confuse, with any other school you subsequently use. In China there is a saying that 'form overrides compass' and I begin every consultation with this basic topographical assessment. There's a big difference between the chi of a basement flat and the chi of a high-rise tower block. The former will require feng shui efforts to ensure the chi doesn't stagnate and accumulate while the latter will require the airy, ungrounded chi to be stabilized and grounded.

SUMMARY

- Ultimately feng shui is about harmonizing the chi flow within a space.

- Form School looks at the landscape for the best 'armchair' position.

- Form School doesn't use complex calculations, the compass directions or the bagua.

- Compass School aligns the bagua with the geographical compass directions and assesses both the time and space of buildings.

- Modern feng shui aligns the bagua with the property's front door.

- Always look at the feng shui 'form' of your property in your initial assessment.

- Choose which school you are going to use to align the bagua and stick to it. If you live in a flat, terrace or semi-detached property use the front door for alignment. If you live in a detached, open, rural situation use the compass directions to align the bagua.

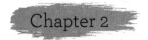

Chapter 2

The Core Principles of Feng Shui

'Generating and nourishing, generating and not possessing, being effective and not retaining, increasing and not dominating: this is the secret of life.'

TAO TE CHING

When we understand the fundamental principles behind how something works, we are able to work in a new way. A cook who knows how to mix together ingredients in a certain way can produce delicious food, but if we don't know the secrets of which foods blend well, and how they work together, we'll create something inedible. The same is true of our homes. If we blend our belongings harmoniously within a space it feels delicious and welcoming when we walk in, and our friends and families will enjoy it too.

Yin and yang

After chi, yin and yang is the next fundamental feng shui principle. If we understand this concept then we can develop the confidence to alter our space intuitively. Yin and yang represent the two primary forces of chi, and this concept has been part of Chinese philosophy, science and medicine for thousands of years. It is the same principle that governs the practice of acupuncture, where yin symbolizes feminine nature – weak and passive – and yang the masculine nature – strong and active. This implies that yin is, perhaps, somehow less than yang but, of course, they are simply two sides of the same coin and life is in constant flux between the two.

> 'The qi of yin and yang breathes out as wind, rises up as clouds, descends as rain, and courses underground as vital energy.'
> THE ZANGSHO

Feng shui is all about finding balance in a constantly fluctuating universe and this is beautifully represented in the ubiquitous yin/yang. The black dot within the white and the white dot within the black symbolizes that we are always wending our way somewhere between yin and yang or yang and yin, moving inexorably from one state to its opposite and back. Within the extreme of one thing is always found its opposite: the cycle of life and of breath, up and down, in and out, down and up, out and in. Navigating this tension between freedom and control, limitlessness and limits is the ultimate challenge for us all. By bringing together the fixed and the fluid, we give birth to flexibility.

For us to be able to work our feng shui magic, initially we need to focus on understanding more about the fluctuating nature of these two primary energies, yin and yang, and also the third force, the chi, that drives them.

Life is a constant dance between yin and yang to dominate and control. The point of harmony is the balance between these two opposing forces. This balance is not a static state but rather a constant pulse of microscopic oscillations. Everything in life, in nature, our own biology, is always attempting to maintain, or return to, a state of homeostasis or balance. This is what we're seeking to achieve in our homes too, with some living spaces being more suited to lively yang energy, e.g. living rooms, and some being more suited to calmer yin energy, e.g. bedrooms.

Case study

One male client had many power struggles and general conflict showing up in his life. On visiting his home it was clear why. It was an extremely yang environment with black and red as the predominant colours. There were crossed swords over the bed, spiky curtain rails and spears on the wall, and generally a lot of sharp, aggressive placements. By softening the edges of his home, you might say we feminized it, thereby adding yin and restoring balance. As a result his interactions with others similarly softened.

Signs and symptoms

We can begin to recognize the yin and yang energies of our decor by learning some of the common associations of both forces.

Yang qualities	Yin qualities
Masculine	Feminine
Active	Receptive
Dynamic	Nurturing
Heaven force	Earth force
Daytime	Night-time
Summer	Winter
Light	Dark
Conscious	Unconscious
Sun	Moon
Fire	Water
South	North
Midday	Midnight
Reason	Imagination

Yang energies	Yin energies
Living	Death
Dancing	Inertia
Working	Creativity
Manic energy	Stillness
Outward	Inward
Speed	Slowness
Active	Lack of motivation
Sports	Reading, sleeping and resting, listening to music
Physical manifestation	Meditation
Full moon – loud, sociable, etc.	New moon – quiet, introverted, etc.
Logic	Intuition

Yang associations	Yin associations
Deserts, large skies, open fields	Condensed, contracted spaces, swampy, dark
Open spaces	Closed spaces
Upward moving	Downward moving
Sharp objects	Soft, no definition
Straight, vertical lines	Curved, flowing environments
Hot, bright colours, lots of red and black	Bland, washed-out colours
Hot, busy environments (good for offices)	Cool, still environments (better for bedrooms for a good night's sleep)
Aggressive or conflicting patterns (e.g. patterned wallpaper and patterned carpets combined, often used in transitory places such as hotels)	Too many mirrors, especially if they are opposite each other, creating confusion and lack of focus
Natural and bright lights	Soft lighting and shadows
Overly masculine environments	Overly feminine environments
Hot, dry environments	Watery environments

Feng shui key

Remember nothing is ever fully yang or fully yin.

The third force – chi

Without the third influence, yin would be yin and yang would be yang, sitting side by side, yet they are constantly moving. The third energy is the world of invisible chi – the force that moves all in the universe and contains all in the universe. This is the intangible energy we are coming to terms with recognizing and experiencing in our homes.

Exercise: Finding the yin–yang balance

Walk round your home with the above lists of yin and yang correspondences. Can you see the interplay of yin and yang? Look at your bedroom – this room should be predominantly yin, as you want to sleep and be receptive here, whereas your living room should be slightly more yang so that you feel energized to socialize and enjoy life.

Change is constant

Feng shui is often portrayed as a one-off exercise that once done will enable you to get on with living the perfect life. Now you understand a little about yin and yang, you can perhaps see that it's not as simple as that. Balancing your home is not a static practice; it is about relationships. Your home is alive, as are you, and it is how you interact with your space on a daily basis that bears fruit. Our homes mirror and reflect our life experiences, and these are constantly changing and evolving, and feng shui likewise is a continuous process.

Feng shui key

Feng shui is always changing – a vase of flowers here, a particular picture or ornament there – that's the approach that keeps us in harmony with the in-breath and out-breath of daily life.

In terms of our yin/yang, feng shui is about restoring and maintaining balance. If something's too sharp, add softness. Too cold, warm it up with soft furnishings, colour or textiles. Too dark, add light. Too bright, add some shade or curtains. Too stuffy, open the windows and clear the clutter.

Exercise: Feeling the energy of your home

Close your eyes and visit your home in your imagination. Wander from room to room, pausing as you reach the centre of each room. If you had to name the quality or essence of the predominant feeling of the room, what would it be? Make notes in your journal afterwards of what you experienced.

Use these qualities to make changes. For example, if a room felt depressing, what could you add to cheer it up? If it felt sad, what would bring joy? If it felt dirty or stagnant, maybe it needs a spring clean. If the energy felt transitory, what could you add to represent stability – a statue, for example, or a piece of square, earthy furniture?

Feng shui key

Making changes little and often is better than all at once.

The five elements

Understanding the five elements is the next master feng shui principle. They represent the backbone of feng shui from both a modern and a classical perspective.

In 2,600BCE The Yellow Emperor wrote the original treatise on Traditional Chinese Medicine (TCM) called *Nei Ching*. In it he introduced a deeper look at the yin/yang cycle and included the five stages of transformation, or elements, that make up the universe. These basic building blocks are: water, wood, fire, earth, metal.

All matter falls into one or a combination of these categories. An understanding of how these five elements interrelate helps us create change by adjusting the element balance of our homes to increase beneficial sheng chi and reduce harmful sha chi. These five phases are an integral part of how the yin and yang energies are physically expressed.

The ancient Chinese believed that these five phases and their varied interactions gave rise to all manifested form in the universe. The five individual energies can be expressed thus:

- **Fire:** Radiates outwards; full peak of expression
- **Earth:** Downwards; compacting, grounding
- **Metal:** Inwards; contracting, consolidating
- **Water:** Floating, falling; dormant
- **Wood:** Upwards; growth, birth

Exercise: Tuning in to the elements

Close your eyes and relax before bringing to mind each element in turn: wood, fire, earth, metal and water. With each element spend a few minutes exploring its nature and different forms. For example, you might imagine walking through a wood, feeling into the nature of the trees, then picking up a fallen log from the forest floor and smelling it, touching it, observing it. Take that log to a fire and watch it burn. Do a similar process for each of the other elements.

Document your findings in your journal. The more you can tune in to the essence of each element, truly understanding its nature, the more you'll become familiar with its particular transformative power and will be able to recognize these powers at work within your home.

Good feng shui requires a balance of these five elements, both within a home and within a room. We feel naturally more comfortable in a balanced environment, or one that veers slightly towards a predominance of wood or water elements. Again these elemental interactions are an organic living process, they are not static, and the nature of their relationship changes as we change. Feng shui considers the relationship between the elements rather than the essence of any one particular element. It is this changing, interactive and transformative nature to which we need to pay attention. Most objects contain a mixture of elements, not just one. The mixture can also change form as, for example, water can manifest as ice, snow, raindrops, mist and steam – all forms of water but in different manifestations of chi.

- Too much earth leads to stagnation and clutter.

- Too much water leads to confusion, isolation and lack of focus.

- Too much wood leads to rigidity.

- Too much fire can lead to erratic, scattered energies and burnout.

- Too much metal can lead to judgement, conflict and withdrawal.

Are the elements in your home feeding or controlling each other?

The five elements interact with each other in specific ways. Wood feeds fire by providing fuel, fire feeds earth by burning wood down to ashes, which renew earth; earth feeds metal by creating the immense force required for metal to form;

metal feeds water through condensation; water feeds wood enabling it to grow; conversely, fire controls metal by melting it. Earth controls water by creating structures to contain it and soak it up. Metal controls wood by chopping it down with axes and saws. Water controls fire by putting it out and wood controls earth by disrupting it with its roots. The diagrams below illustrate these cycles.

The productive/nourishing cycle

In this cycle, each element feeds the next in a generative, harmonious relationship. It is known as the 'mother–son' relationship, where each element is the mother of the one it produces and the son of the one that produces it.

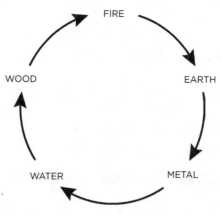

The productive cycle

The controlling cycle

Often described as the destructive cycle, this doesn't accurately describe the true nature of these relationships. They are not destroying each other but rather honing or containing each other. Energy cannot be destroyed; it simply changes form. If the controlling cycle is strong within an environment, it will cause a build-up of stagnant or sha chi, as no growth is possible in this cycle. In cases where there is too much of a good thing, however, then the controlling cycle can be used effectively. Think of a bush fire, for example, in which fire is feeding the earth but in an uncontrolled way. The firefighters add water to control the fire. In this instance the controlling element becomes part of the solution and is very helpful. They also use earth walls and ditches to drain the fire by cutting off its fuel supply; see the reductive cycle (*page 38*).

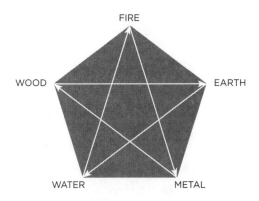

The controlling cycle

Originally there were four elements – wood, fire, water and metal – each associated with one of the four cardinal directions, and earth was placed in the middle. These teachings consolidated into the Five Elements Form – used today – during the Han Dynasty. (206BCE to AD220). During this period the five elements were integrated into the lo shu square, which we'll explore, together with the eight trigrams, in more detail in Chapter 3.

The weakening or reductive cycle
Within these five transformations, there is a third cycle: the counter-clockwise 'weakening' or 'reductive' cycle. This is where wood reduces water by absorbing it; water reduces metal through corrosion; metal reduces earth through compression; earth reduces fire by production of ashes; fire reduces wood through utilizing its fuel.

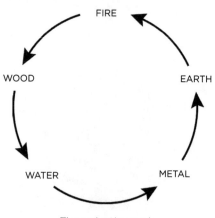

The reductive cycle

This cycle is sometimes overlooked but it is key to making elemental changes. For example, perhaps you notice that your living room has a predominance of metal and fire: fire controls metal. It seems reasonable to add water to control the fire. But water reduces metal and would then gain control itself. The best element to add would be earth. This element will reduce the controlling fire and strengthen the weakened metal, thereby restoring harmony. To take another example, you notice your bedroom has a predominance of wood and earth: wood controls earth. You may be tempted to add metal to control the wood. But metal reduces the weakened earth and takes control. A better option is to add fire, which will reduce the controlling wood and feed the weakened earth.

Walk around your home room by room, while using the table below to check the element balance in each room. Notice the wood shapes, the earth, metal, fire and water elements. Write down your findings. Is there a pattern emerging? What changes would support you?

Fire	Purple, red colour spectrum; diamond shapes and triangles; electrical items, e.g. TVs, radios, stereos, etc.; candles, lights, fireplaces, red lampshades
	Fire feeds earth, drains wood and controls metal.
Earth	Yellow, orange, brown colour spectrum; crystals, rocks, statues, tiled floors, ceramics; square, squat furniture, e.g. brown leather sofas; plants (with the exception of bamboo, which is more wood energy)
	Earth feeds metal, drains fire and controls water.
Metal	Gold, silver, white, bronze, copper metallic colour spectrum; metal frames and appliances; oval, circular and arch shapes found in the decor and/or picture frames, filing cabinets, metallic wind chimes, etc.
	Metal feeds water, drains earth and controls wood.
Water	Blue, black colour spectrum; inorganic shapes, e.g. beanbags, sheepskin rugs etc.; water features: ponds, fish tanks, fountains etc.; paintings of seascapes and other watery places
	Water feeds wood, drains metal and controls fire
Wood	Full green colour spectrum; upward-growing plants, e.g. bamboo; tall wooden furniture; uplighters, standing lamps, tall slim vases and ornaments; paintings of forests and trees, etc.
	Wood feeds fire, drains water and controls earth

At this stage we're collecting evidence and ideas for change, and maybe there are some obvious things you might want to change straight away. But for now, just enjoy being the detective of your life and investigating the space you live in and what it is reflecting back to you. When making element changes, it is important to be aware that size does matter. If you have a predominance of wood in a room due to large plants and furniture and the room is also painted green this would be referred to as 'big wood'. Adding 'small fire', a single candle for example, to drain the wood in this instance wouldn't work because the elemental balance needs to be harmonious in terms of size. Although, remember that with the fire element less is always more, as you will always need more wood to fuel a fire. This might seems like a lot of information to take on board right away but as you progress through the following chapters, you'll find that you become increasingly aware of these subtle differences.

There are two fundamental ways of identifying the element chi of any object. First ask yourself what it is made of, and second, what it symbolizes. For example, a bamboo picture frame belongs to wood, while a gold frame will be metal. In the same way ask yourself what a rock symbolizes? Obviously the earth, so it represents the earth element. And what does a whale symbolize? They live in the ocean therefore whales symbolize the water element.

Cycles and spirals

Nothing in nature has a straight line and similarly chi moves in spirals and rhythmic cycles. Notice how dust and cobwebs (signs of stagnant sha chi) always collect in corners. Attuning ourselves to these natural cycles improves our general wellbeing and brings us into a natural flow with life and nature – and that's the best feng shui of all.

We ignore this sense of cyclical rhythm to our detriment. We're taught that to get ahead we have to take action, make quick decisions. We're constantly seeking progress, often pushing ourselves to work harder and harder to accomplish more and more. But if we pause and look around, we become aware that the natural world is in a constant cycle, evolving and progressing, seemingly quite effortlessly. In our lives too, there is a cycle for making progress AND for letting go. Tune in to you. Work with your natural cycles using nature as your guide. You can use the seasons or the rhythms of the moon or both.

Seasonal changes

We are naturally more energetic during spring. This is the real New Year for me and is when the feng shui New Year begins too. It makes far more sense to set resolutions then than on 1 January when the earth's energies are still dormant. In spring, we respond to the earth's active energies beneath our feet. The chi is expanding as the bulbs begin to erupt, the blossom buds and the earth goes full tilt into her growth spurt. If we're in tune with our environment, we notice that we suddenly want to move more, get out and about. We're emerging from our winter hibernation. Often we might feel as though we're starting afresh at this time. We feel the urge to clean our homes (hence the tradition of spring cleaning) and clear clutter. We're responding to the earth's urge to shake off the winter stagnation and create space for the new to emerge. It can also be a time of frenetic, scattered energy. We haven't set our course in stone yet. It's a time for exploring what's on offer, checking things out, networking, trying new things.

As we move into summer, activity is at its height. This is not the urgent growth of spring but rather a maturing energy. Flowers are in full bloom while fruits and crops are ripening in the full summer sun. We feel the need to be outdoors more. We want to share our energy with others. We feel buoyant and abundant. Next comes autumn, a time of contraction and consolidation: a shift in emphasis towards harvesting what we have sown. While winter sees the leaves fall from the trees and the earth become still and quiet. It's not completely inactive though. It's in a period of repose and reflection. True creativity comes from this place of stillness. We need to shed the old and outdated in order to allow space for the new to come in the next spring spurt.

Moon magic

We can also work on smaller, monthly, moon cycles (*see page 229 for a digital moon cycle almanac*). The few days leading up to a new moon are low in energy. This is a time for reflection and contemplation, rather than to hold a wild party or sign a top deal. The new moon itself heralds the beginning of the new cycle. New moons are great for starting projects and planting crops, and if you're growing your hair it's the best time for a haircut.

The period between a new moon and a full moon is the growth spurt, a time to forge ahead with plans, call people, set up meetings, start a new fitness regime – basically take action on all levels. As you near the full moon, this active energy reaches its zenith. This is a well-researched phenomenon and the police and the emergency services put extra staff on duty around this time, as the full moon energy can lead to more accidents than usual. It's a great time for a party though, as the energy will be high and everyone will be feeling sociable, which will collectively make it a success.

Just after the full moon is a time to evaluate and see what is no longer working. What can you delegate? What do you need to change? What no longer serves you? Those days just before the new moon are perhaps the deadest of the month and the most productive you can be at this time is literally to throw out your clutter, contemplate and prepare the way for the cycle to begin again.

Exercise: Working with moon cycles

Try working to the moon cycles for a few months, working with their energy rather than against it and see what a difference it makes to your general wellbeing and your productivity levels. My guess is after a few months you won't want to revert back to your old, unaware patterns.

Even the days of the week, although man-made, have a rhythm to them. Sunday is a day for reflection and contemplation of the week ahead. Monday is like the new moon, we feel a bit sluggish but we plan our week ahead and put things in place. By Wednesday we're in full swing and achieving our objectives (just like the height of the full moon) but by Thursday we're beginning to flag or are running to the finish line. By Friday we're looking forward to a rest. Saturday is time for chores and clearing out the week's junk and then back to Sunday.

Now you've got a grip on the basic underlying principles, we can move on to the juicy part of learning how to lay the bagua over your home and find out where all your feng shui hot spots are and what to do about them.

SUMMARY

- Yin and yang symbolize the constant motion of chi – everything is alive, connected and changing.

- Balancing yin and yang is the primary purpose of feng shui – everything seeks a state of homeostasis.

- Is your home too yang? Add some soft feminine touches, such as textiles, cushions and throws. Neutralize the colour scheme and avoid harsh patterns.

- Is your home too yin? Add some bright colours and bold patterns. Add structure and sharp lines.

- Check your five elements – are they in balance? Need growth? Add some water and wood elements. Out of control and confused? Reduce wood and add metal. Feeling stuck? Add some water and wood and reduce earth. (*For more ideas on elemental changes see page 65.*)

- Check your rhythms – which cycle are you in right now? Birthing, ripening, maturing or letting go?

Chapter 3

Life Evaluation and the Bagua

*'The least of things with a meaning
is worth more in life than the
greatest of things without it.'*

CARL JUNG, *MODERN MAN IN SEARCH OF A SOUL*

Next it's time to look at the role of metaphor in your home. This is of primary importance as you continue your feng shui journey. Always keep in the back of your mind, what is the story my home is telling me? What patterns can I see emerging? As you're discovering, we can understand our internal world by conscious, detached observation of our external world. Everything is a reflection of our internal reality and so feng shui can be like therapy in reverse. Modern feng shui has developed an edge in focusing on this concept of environmental psychology. Often it is easier to create initial change by working from the outside in than the inside out. We can use the metaphors we uncover in our homes to create more obvious 'ah-ha' moments and get a clearer understanding of our blocks and ourselves. We can then move or add items in our homes to create the necessary changes in metaphoric chi we need in our lives.

Case study

An example of metaphors at work is a client who came to me because she had been single for eight years and was desperate for a relationship. Visiting her home, I noticed that she slept in a narrow single bed and had portraits of single women hung in prominent places but, most telling of all, she had a picture of Jesus Christ, a statue of the Buddha and a postcard of the Pope in her relationships corner (you'll discover where this is later in this chapter). I simply asked her how great she thought their sex lives were. She 'got it' and immediately moved these symbols to a more appropriate area. Before the end of the consultation, a man knocked on the door. This woman lived in the middle of nowhere, at the end of a long, winding lane and in the 10 years she had lived in the house had never had an unexpected visitor – a fabulous sign that her relationship issue had shifted and needless to say she didn't remain single for long.

Seeing the metaphors and symbols in your home

When 'reading' houses I look for what repeats, stands out and is exaggerated. One of anything is fine but ten of something needs investigating. For example, one client had a small cottage and 12 clocks, none of which told the right time. She also had a large collection of old-fashioned desk calendars with roll dials, each displaying a different date, month and year. She had written on her pre-consultation questionnaire, 'I have no time.'

Pay attention to the words you use to describe life in your home because those external signs will have an impact on your life whether you like it or not. For example, another client had a house full of dinosaur parts. Her young son was a keen enthusiast and his passion was indulged. When I asked the client what was wrong she said, 'I feel since I moved here that my social life has become *extinct*.' Symbolism and imagery hold vital clues to your inner world. Look at your home with fresh eyes. See the story it is revealing to you.

Case study

One client explained her problem, as 'I cannot connect with my work; every time I try to do some writing on the computer I get stuck.' When I viewed her office it was easy to see why. Her desk was in the loft – a large airy room and rather lovely, but her desk was positioned directly under a large galvanized-steel supporting beam. As she reached forwards to the keyboard, this beam literally 'cut' her off from her work. The solution was easy; we moved the desk further out from under the beam and the client immediately reported that she was able to connect with her work.

Another client had a similar issue, except he was also suffering with major depression. He lived in a stunning, five-storey London townhouse yet had chosen to place his desk in a basement office facing away from the garden with his head positioned under the main supporting beam for the entire house – sitting at that desk over time would be enough to give most people depression! It really can be that simple sometimes. The story of our life lives in what we surround ourselves with. If you're happy with the story, great; if not, what can you change in your home that will help change the story?

Walk around your home reviewing your choice of artwork, ornaments, paintings and photos. What metaphors can you see around your home? Are they vibrant and alive or dark and dank? Do they make you feel good? Or are they confusing abstracts without focus that might be making it difficult for you to complete things? Are there scenes of natural beauty or industrial decay? Think about what was happening in your life at the time you bought the item – is that still in alignment with where you are now? Or where you're heading? Look for recurring themes and symbols that repeat. If they represent your current life and you're happy with that – great; if they don't, consider changing them for something that supports your vision of the future. You might also want to invite a friend round and ask them what their answers to these questions are.

How to do feng shui

Feng shui is all about attitude. Be alert. Be curious. Look around your home, with new eyes, as if for the first time. Instead of jumping straight in with the bagua, the energetic map at the heart of feng shui, it's good to start by connecting with the raw, unconscious energy of your home as it is, feeling into what lies just under the surface. Good feng shui is 90 per cent observation and only 10 per cent solutions and cures.

Exercise: Meditation journey

The following meditation journey can help you connect to your home and gain a new understanding of it. You may like to record it first with suitable pauses, so that you can just relax and listen while it plays back or you can read it through once and allow your intuition to guide you on the journey through your home. Whichever way you choose, it's best performed away from your home, maybe at a friend's house or somewhere outside in nature, but if that proves difficult do it in your garden or a room that isn't your regular haunt. You also need to be somewhere comfortable where you won't be disturbed for half an hour or so. Have your journal with you and some colouring pens and pencils.

Start by making yourself comfortable and allow yourself to become empty and receptive by focusing on your natural breathing for a few minutes; just observing your breath, not trying to change it in any way.

Feel the gentle gravitational pull of the earth below you. It's very comforting to feel how we are magnetically attached to the planet.

Now imagine yourself walking along the street to your home. See yourself approaching the front door of your home. Look around. What do you feel? What do you hear? What do you see? What gets your attention as you walk towards your house?

Just observe rather than judge what happens. There is no right and wrong, there just is.

Open your front door and walk into your hallway, closing the door behind you. Pause for a moment. How does it feel to be home? What emotions or feelings are present as you stand in your hallway?

Continue this process right through your home. There's only your own path to follow but make sure you visit each area. Where do you automatically want to head for once inside? What's there? Who's there?

Again what do you feel, hear, see, notice, maybe even smell? Wander slowly around the inside of your home visiting each room, feeling what you feel, hearing what you hear, seeing what you see and noticing what you notice. Observe your body language as you move from room to room. Do you hesitate anywhere? Is there a room you quickly move on from? Is there any room or area where you don't want to linger?

When you've finished, walk to the front door and leave, thanking your home for the insights and secrets it has offered up to you. Slowly bring your awareness back into your body, stretch a few times and wriggle your toes. Before speaking to anyone, record in your journal anything that particularly struck you and anything else that was of meaning to you – perhaps there was a colour that sprang to mind when you entered a room or an idea for decoration. Also consider the answers to the following questions.

❖ What is the most important room in my home for me?

❖ Where in that room do I like to sit?

❖ Where is the heart of my home?

❖ Where do I spend most time in my home?

❖ Where do I feel most safe in my home?

You'll have discovered that your home is remarkably chatty for a supposedly inanimate object! We'll come back to these answers in a while. But first, there are two keys to bear in mind when mastering feng shui changes:

Feng shui key

'Less is more' and 'If it ain't broke, don't fix it.'

Looking at your life balance

The following feng shui life-balance questionnaire can help you focus on your priorities for change because if you change everything at once you'll create chaos. Good feng shui is about creating a harmonious relationship between all the elements. Similarly, if after laying the bagua later in this chapter, you discover your wealth/blessings area is 'missing' yet you have great wealth, then leave well alone.

Exercise: Life-balance questionnaire

It's important to record your answers to the life-balance questionnaire, so turn to a blank page in your journal and draw a vertical line down its centre to create two columns. Give the first column the heading 'How is this area of my life now?' and the second column 'How would I like it to be?' Now answer the following questions using the scale 1–10, where 1 is awful and 10 is fabulous, Don't spend time thinking, just write down the first two numbers that come into your head for each of the nine questions – your instinctive responses. If you overthink it, the questions may confuse you as you think of more and more possibilities or ways to answer them. It is that instant response that counts.

1. **Career/life path** (*progression, journey in life, etc.*): Do you love what you do? Are you passionate about your work? Or are you stuck in a rut, unfulfilled, frustrated?

2. **Relationships** (*with your spouse, partner, business partner, boss, etc.*): Do you argue constantly or are you single, looking for love? Do you consider yourself part of a well-functioning team? Are you happily married?

3. **Ancestors/family** (*with parents, grandparents, siblings, teachers, mentors, etc.*): Do you get on well with your family? Do you have

strong mentors that you feel supported by? Did you hate school? Are you estranged from family?

4. **Wealth/blessings** (*fortune, luck, abundance, etc.*): Do you consider yourself a lucky person? Do you feel blessed that opportunities tend to turn up when you need them? Or do you feel everyone has more luck than you or that you never quite get to cross the finish line?

5. **Health** (*wellbeing, energy, vitality, etc.*): Do you generally feel alive and full of energy or do you find it hard to drag yourself out of bed in the morning? Do you suffer any kind of dis-ease or trauma?

6. **Helpful friends/travel** (*charity, community service, etc.*): Are you willing to lend a hand when needed? Are there always friends on tap when you need them?

7. **Creativity/children** (*ideas, projects, offspring, etc.*): Are you fully expressing yourself? Do you love your children? Do you have healthy relationships with your children? Are you experiencing difficulties conceiving? Do your projects succeed?

8. **Self-development** (*meditation, spiritual development, etc.*): Do you know what makes you tick? Do you spend quality time with yourself? Do you have a daily practice?

9. **Fame/reputation** (*placement in social hierarchy, relationship to peers, etc.*): Do you feel your worth is recognized in the world? Are you respected, valued and well paid for what you do? Do you care what people think of you?

Use your three lowest scores to prioritize which areas you need to work on first and make sure you note them in your journal.

You'll be using this information a little later in this chapter when we start looking at using the principles of feng shui to make adjustments in your own home.

I Ching

Whether science can prove the presence of chi or not, the Chinese absolutely believed in its existence and spent many millennia studying its form carefully. Through careful observation, predictable patterns of chi flow were documented. Legend has it that the original eight trigrams, or basic energies, from which all else comes, were discovered by Fu Hsi watching a turtle emerge from the Lo River. The unusual and distinctive patterns on the turtle's shell seemed to reflect the primary universal patterns of chi. These became the eight primary trigrams that form the basis of the 64 hexagrams of the *I Ching*, which effectively depicts every chi mutation possible between yin and yang and back again. This book underpins all Chinese Taoist disciplines including feng shui.

Feng shui key

The Chinese studied the transformation and movement of chi, not its static nature. They understood it was a constantly moveable feast.

To understand the bagua it's good to have at least a basic knowledge of the symbols associated with the eight-trigram family that make-up the 64 hexagrams of the *I Ching*. The following table shows the basic correspondences for the eight trigrams.

There are nine areas associated with our feng shui map, but only eight trigrams because the ninth, central area is the transformational pivot. It has no trigram of its own as it represents the 'tai chi' – the perfect balance between yin and yang. This is why it represents health, as without good health it is difficult to achieve balance in the other life areas.

Trigram	Family member and bagua house	Colour and shape	Element and direction
Heaven ☰	Father/Chien 6. Helpful friends/travel	White, gold, silver, bronze Circle, arch, ellipse	Metal North west
Thunder ☳	Eldest Son/Chen 3. Ancestors/family	Dark green Oblong, rectangle	Wood East
Water ☵	Middle Son/Kan 1. Career/life path	Blue, black Organic, flowing	Water North
Mountain ☶	Youngest Son/Ken 8. Self-development	Purple, mauve, maroon Square, squat	Earth North east
Tai Chi – Centre ☯	No family member 5. Health	Yellow, primrose Square, squat	Earth Centre
Earth ☷	Mother/Kun 2. Relationships	Peach, orange Square, squat	Earth South west

Trigram	Family member and bagua house	Colour and shape	Element and direction
Wind ☴	Eldest Daughter/ Sun 4. Wealth/ blessings	Light Green Oblong, rectangle	Wood South east
Fire ☲	Middle Daughter/ Li 9. Fame/ reputation	Red, purple Triangle, diamond, star	Fire South
Lake ☱	Youngest Daughter/Tui 7. Creativity/ children	White, gold, silver, bronze Circle, arch, ellipse	Metal West

The bagua

The Chinese mapped these eight trigrams on a grid, which became known as the feng shui bagua: an eight-sided map with 'ba' meaning eight and 'gua' meaning sector or area. It acts as a template that can be laid over a plot of land, a floor plan, a room or even an individual desk.

Confusion sometimes arises due to the different names given to describe the bagua but they refer to the same thing. In classical feng shui they call it the pa kua. It is also sometimes confused with the lo shu, the magic square. Certainly in modern contexts, the lo shu and the bagua are used almost interchangeably.

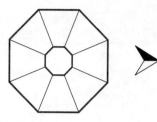 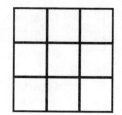

Bagua/pa kua

Magic square or lo shu

The magic square or lo shu

4	9	2
3	5	7
8	1	6

Chinese philosophy sees the magic square or lo shu as representing the pattern of life itself and developed an entire cosmology around unlocking its mysteries. The lo shu dates back to at least 650BCE and its magic lies in the fact that whichever way you add the rows of numbers – horizontally, vertically or diagonally – the result is always 15. 15, divided by the number of rows (three), is five, the number of transformation in the centre.

Early and Later Heaven Sequences

To complicate matters further there are two versions of the bagua – the Early Heaven Sequence and the Later Heaven Sequence.

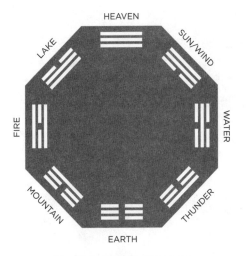

HEAVEN

LAKE

SUN/WIND

FIRE

WATER

MOUNTAIN

THUNDER

EARTH

The Early Heaven Sequence

The Early Heaven Sequence is an image of heaven's perfection before the phenomenal world came into being. As you can see all the elements are perfectly balanced and in harmony with each other as pairs of opposites. This sequence creates a neutral, perfected state of balance but, as we know, life itself is in a perpetual state of motion. The Later Heaven Sequence illustrates how chi flows, accumulates, transforms and disperses through time and space. This is the trigram layout we use in feng shui (see chart on next page).

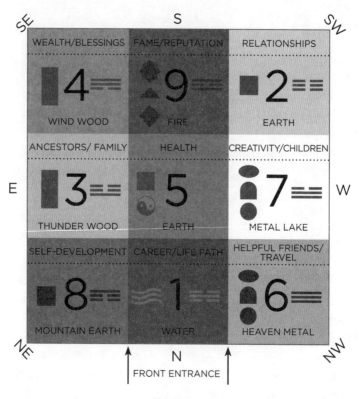

The bagua

Each of the nine areas of this bagua has a set of characteristics and qualities. Each area, except for the centre (health), has been named in accordance with a trigram from the *I Ching* with which it is associated. The centre square (health) is the equivalent to the void – it's the emptiness that makes the rest work. Think of a wheel; it needs to have a hole in the middle in order to function. Each square is also given one of the first nine cardinal numbers.

Exercise: Mapping your home

Devising a treasure map utilizing the nine areas of the bagua can help you create a new reality more aligned to your purpose. On a large piece of paper use symbols, words, and drawings to create a collage of what you want in your life. For example, if you'd like more help on certain projects put a photo of the help or the people you want to provide it in the sixth house (helpful friends/travel area). When the project is finished place your photo somewhere in the ninth house (fame/reputation) of your home.

Placing the bagua over your home

The easiest way to orientate the bagua is to stand at your front door looking into your home. Imagine the space divided into nine squares as if you were playing noughts and crosses. Briefly each space represents the following area of your life:

- The top left-hand corner is your wealth and/or blessings.

- Top middle represents your fame or reputation in life.

- Top right is your relationships; all relationships not just significant others.

- Middle row left-hand side represents your ancestors and family.

- The centre is health.

- Middle row right-hand side is children and creativity.

- Bottom left is your self-development.

- Bottom middle is your career or life path.

- Bottom right is your helpful friends and travel.

In the modern feng shui system we align the bagua so that the front door aligns with the houses 8, 1 or 6. The only exception to this would be if you lived in the middle of the countryside with no neighbours so that your main source of chi was the sun. In this instance use the compass directions of your property to align the bagua rather than the front door. It's easy to do; you simply find north, which represents 1 of the bagua, your career/life path. Stand in that place looking into your home and apply the bagua as above.

You can also place the bagua over individual rooms using the same principle of aligning the main door into the room with the houses 8, 1 or 6. If you use it to feng shui your desk, use where you sit facing the desk as the entrance gate.

Feng shui key

In this system, your front door symbolizes the main source of chi rather than the sun. It is the source of opportunities and flow via visitors and the post, etc. If there is any doubt as to what can be considered the front door, use the door that was architecturally designed to be the front door or the door to which the post gets delivered.

Each floor of a house has the same bagua, i.e. if a bathroom on the ground floor has a bedroom above it they are both considered to be in the same area of the bagua. If you live in a block of flats, orientate the bagua from your personal front door, not the front door of the building. Occasionally if you have an L-shaped house it is possible that your front door may fall in square 7 or 3 of the bagua. It may be that your house is not a perfect square or rectangle, in which case it will have what feng shui calls 'missing areas'. We'll deal with them later but for now just notice which area of the bagua they fall in.

The areas of the bagua may span more than one room or divide a room between two areas. The bagua is not actually a square but an octagonal map and the areas are like cake wedges coming from a central circle – for ease of use and to get you started, using the nine-square layout works just as well. We are not using precise measurements that require a pinpoint accurate bagua placement. I question the necessity of this type of feng shui – I consider the properties of chi to be more fluid and flexible than that.

Sometimes the octagonal bagua grid is easier to use if aligning your home with the compass directions, or if you have an irregularly shaped house, as it fits precisely with the segments of a compass and can be stretched to fit any floor plan. The easiest way to do this is to take a floor plan and draw a diagonal line from corner to corner, as follows:

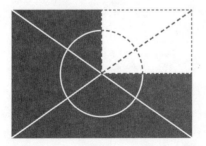

Then place a cross from top to bottom and side to side like so:

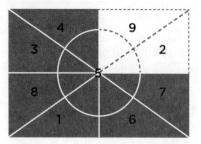

If you look at the bagua chart (*see page 58*) you'll notice each of the squares relates to one of the nine life areas used in the life-balance questionnaire. You can now discover where these same areas are physically located in your home. The dotted lines represent the so-called 'missing areas' so, in our example above, the ninth and second house are 'missing' from the floor plan.

Look back at your three lowest scores from the life-balance questionnaire (*see page 51*) and check with your floor plan to see what area of your home those issues fall into. For example, you may have been single for many years, and when you check you find the whole relationship area of your home is missing. Or finances have been tricky and then you discover that's where your messy, sullen teenager has their bedroom.

Feng shui key

The bagua is just one tool; it's still important to check out the form of your landscape to assess the chi coming in and out of your home.

Most feng shui practitioners, including myself, will also assess the astrology of the residents of a house. As we're learning, feng shui is ALL about relationships: the relationship of the chi, yin and yang, the five elements, the eight trigrams, the nine houses, you and your home, you and life. Both you and your home have electromagnetic fields that need to be in alignment with each other. You cannot assess the feng shui of a building without also having some understanding of the energy of the people who live there and how they interact with that specific building. Traditional feng shui methods include the Flying Stars, 9 Star Ki and the Ming Gua Numbers and the Four Pillars of Destiny (Ba Zi).

Modern practitioners will sometimes use one of these methods; I certainly use 9 Star Ki and the Ming Gua Numbers. I also use Western astrology, as I was an astrologer before I became a feng shui consultant and find the information helpful for clients. A good place to begin is to know your primary astrological element. Are you a fire, water, earth or air sign? Or from a Chinese astrological perspective what element of animal are you – e.g. a fire horse or a metal dragon? (If you know your date of birth you can discover your element through any number of free online Chinese astrology calculators.) From what you've learnt about the elements how does your current home support or hinder your basic element?

These days there is considerable supporting evidence for the efficacy of feng shui, both anecdotal and scientific. If you're still in doubt consider the following.

From nothing (0) the chi flows (1), branching into yang (1) and yin (2), giving rise to the three primary forces (3), ,which disperse and transform into the five elements (5), which move into the eight trigrams (8). Those numbers add up to the basic Fibonacci Sequence of 0, 1, 1, 2, 3, 5, 8. This famous sequence is found everywhere in nature and is one of the fundamental mathematical building blocks of the universe. That's evidence enough for me that if we work with these principles we are guaranteed results.

With this in mind let's move on to the nitty-gritty of planning the changes we're going to make in Chapter 4.

SUMMARY

- Become aware of your home's story. What repeats, what stands out, what's exaggerated?

- Know what areas you are working on. Focus on the three lowest scores from the life-balance questionnaire.

- Lay the bagua over your home aligned with either the front door or the compass directions, depending on which method you choose. Map out the nine areas of your home.

- Evaluate the areas that correspond with your three lowest scores. Use these areas to plan changes as suggested in the next chapter.

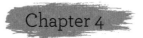

Chapter 4

Introducing the Bagua – House by House

'In all chaos there is a cosmos, in all disorder a secret order.'

CARL JUNG, *ARCHETYPES OF THE COLLECTIVE UNCONSCIOUS*

N ow you've got the basic feng shui tools sorted, we can begin to plan changes relating to the areas you identified as needing assistance in the previous chapter (*see page 51*). You can meander through the nine houses one by one or simply find the ones that correspond to the areas that you wish to enhance and read the suggestions for those. We're still at the planning stage and I'd suggest only implementing your ideas after you read Chapter 5.

It would be impossible to give every permutation of enhancement for each house here. That is limited only by our imaginations. Instead these are suggestions designed to wake up your feng shui imagination. Feel free to use them or make up your own, adhering to the principles of that particular house.

Focus on one or two priority areas at a time. If you change everything all at once you risk creating chaos rather than harmony.

First house: Career/life path (1)

This area governs our life path, career and purpose for being here. When we are fulfilled and passionate about what we do, our lives naturally flow. We automatically attract the right promotions and career progression. Our businesses tend to prosper. Enhance this area if your career needs a boost, you're looking for a new job, you're unhappy at work, or your business has taken a downturn. You can also work on this area if you are lacking in purpose and direction.

First house enhancements

In Chapter 3 we learnt the first house is related to the element of water, which is why you will often see fish tanks in Chinese restaurants. If you do add a fish tank it is better to have an odd number of fish to resonate with the primary number one associated with this house. A cheaper option is to have a picture of fish – again, ensure the image has an odd number of fish. A water feature works well in the first house, as do paintings and photographs of rivers and bridges. It's vital always to think of the nature of the water depicted in the image. Is the river strong and meandering? Does the water look healthy and vibrant? Is it flowing with life towards the sea of expanded consciousness?

A well-lit airy space assists in energizing your career/life path house. By oxygenating the element of water chi in this way, we keep it flowing. Add lights if it is too dark. If appropriate, choose furniture with organic flowing shapes – think watery Monet paintings as a theme, beanbags and soft throws over harsh sofa angles, for example.

Black and blue spectrum watery colours are the official palettes for this house. A bay window or porch can enhance this area when kept clean and beautiful.

Placements to avoid in the first house

Avoid too much earth by making minimum use of yellow and orange earth colours or heavy, square, low-sitting earthy furniture. Earth controls water, and while we need earth's structure to guide the course of our rivers, by providing strong banks, when starting out, we need to be expansive and creative, and excess earth can keep us stuck and muddy in our thinking. Avoid inappropriate artworks such as stagnant water, pools, ponds and lakes – which will lead to career stagnation. Similarly avoid waterfalls and white-water rapids, which can cause work stress as everything crashes and moves too fast, or pictures of the sea where you fall prey to the ebb and flow of the tides.

Artwork is largely dependent on how you interpret it, of course. A good question to ask yourself is, 'What does this mean to me?' I had one client, a landlady, whose tenants seemed to be always suing her or she had to sue them. In the entrance hall, which fell in the first house, she had a huge painting of a waterfall. This crashing energy dominated the space – however, she loved the painting and was reluctant to give it up. We moved it to her bathroom, which fell in her wealth house. Admittedly, this wasn't the best placement, but it was the best compromise.

Remember feng shui is all about relationships and, as we know, relationships require compromise to ensure continuing harmony. In the landlady's house, the idea behind moving the painting was to use its stimulating water energy to stir up any stagnant bathroom chi and feed the wood energy of her wealth. Some months later she reported that all the court cases had been completed, no new ones had arisen and life generally was calmer.

Second house: Relationships (2)

This house governs all significant relationships such as business partners, not just romantic partners. If you're arguing or falling out with people, there's a lot of conflict in your life or you're single and looking for a relationship then this is the house you need to address. Our primary feng shui focus is to look at the area of our home where the second house falls. However, I think it's also good feng shui to look at the main bedroom as well (*see also page 154–161, for specific bedroom advice*). Hopefully this is where you're conducting a great relationship. If you're reluctantly single, assess your bedroom feng shui to see if you're open to receiving love.

Second house enhancements

The magic number of this house is two, the number of relationships. Check your second house. Are there pairs of things? Photographs of you as a couple (preferably looking at each other) or of pairs generally? I have often gone to homes where a person is looking for a relationship, or a relationship has broken down, and all I can see is artwork and ornaments of single people, isolated items or barren landscapes.

One of my favourite relationship enhancements for those looking for a relationship but not yet in one is an image of a pair of pears – this gives a nice play on words (a perfect pair/pear) as well as the imagery doubling the enhancement effect. Another for adding spice to a dwindling sex life is a pair of red-hot chilli peppers. Matching ornaments also work well as do a pair of candlesticks, etc.

However, do be wary with how you place objects. Too often I see separation created by people placing matching ornaments at opposite ends of a mantelshelf. This may create design symmetry but it also creates separation. It is far better to have matching pairs of items together opposite another matching pair, even if those opposing pairs don't match. Relationship chi is relatively easy to implement through imagery and ornaments but there are other options. You could use a pair of square, squat, earthy chairs with matching orange or yellow cushions, for example; a couple of earth-coloured floor cushions to lounge around on or a pair of heart-shaped pieces of rose quartz crystal.

Is there a place where you can sit and chat together, and preferably eat together, in the second house? This is vitally important, as good communication is the glue that keeps relationships alive and healthy. If this isn't possible, due to the physical location of your second house – perhaps because it is in the utility room, for example – then choose another room, such as the living room or dining room and create a special area for eating and sitting within the second house of that particular room.

The best colour activator of relationship chi is the earth range from magnolia and cream through peach tones to orange and yellow to terracotta and chocolate, although adding a little passion with a few touches of fire energy in the form of red, or hot pink or purple is also beneficial. Some candlelight will work equally well as fire feeds earth.

Placements to avoid in the second house

Look at the symbols reflected in your artwork and photos. These should be symbolic of how you want your relationship to be. A photograph of a pair of ferocious tigers in the bedroom will lead to conflict and arguments. I've seen this placement on more than one occasion, if not tigers then some other ferocious beast such as a lion or a pack of wolves, in situations where relationships are strained and full of anger. Avoid lots of single symbolism, such as photos with just one person in them, paintings of empty landscapes, or single ornaments. They are constantly reflecting back to you your single status and if you're in a relationship will cause it to deteriorate, as you both become more singular in your pursuits or reinforce your sense of aloneness.

Wood controls the flow of earth so avoid an overabundance of wood energy in the second house. Limit the number of tall leafy plants, uplighters and bulky wooden furniture in this area. Metal drains earth and too much fire will make it harder for the beneficial relationship chi to flow unhindered.

Third house: Ancestors/family (3)

This is the house of our ancestry, our lineage. We stand on the shoulders of others to be where we are; parents, grandparents, teachers, mentors, advisors, spiritual teachers, guides, etc. Do you honour your ancestors? Respect and acknowledge your teachers? If you're estranged from your family in any way or there are unresolved traumas lurking there, if you struggle to feel supported by mentors or guides in your life, this is the house to address.

Third house enhancements

Rich deep greens are the primary colour of the third house. Think ancient British woodland, ivy, moss, ferns and piles of leaves. Pictures, paintings, ornaments or other representations of trees work well because they remind us of the universal tree of life, as well as family roots and the family tree. The third house is the place for your photographs of family, ancestors, grandparents, teachers and mentors, including spiritual teachers. Tall, upright pieces of wooden furniture are well placed here and it would be the perfect location for any wooden heirlooms. Water features are beneficial as the water element feeds the wood of this house.

Specific placements to avoid in the third house

Be mindful of excess fire and metal energy in the third house. Metal controls wood and can cause family rifts and disagreements. Check your decor for round or oval, gold- or silver-framed mirrors for example. Too many arches or curves in the architectural style will have the same effect.

Fire uses up wood's energy so limit the number of lights and candles and other fire symbols you have in the third house, although a little fire energy is OK. The best light for this area is natural light from a window rather than artificial light, and a single candle that is ritually lit with an acknowledgement to your ancestors, those that have walked before. This can be as simple as just lighting the candle and saying thank you or it can be a more elaborate prayer that you feel inspired to recite.

Here's a great remedy for healing family rifts. Take three separate plant pots (three being the cardinal number of the third house), plant three seeds or three bulbs, one in each pot, and leave these plants to grow on a windowsill in the third house of your home. If this isn't possible because it happens to fall in a windowless stairwell, for example, then choose a windowsill in the third house area of another room, the living room for instance. Nurture the plants with love and care. By the time they bloom you should witness a positive shift in the family dynamic. Even if you remain estranged you will have released any unhelpful emotions around the situation and be able to accept it for what it is. Should the plants die, replace them and start again. You can make this cure more powerful by planting the seeds in conjunction with a new moon.

Fourth house: Wealth/blessings (4)

Known as the house of prosperity it is important to understand that this does not necessarily equate to the money you have in your bank account. True wealth comes in many forms. For me, this house is more about luck. Do you feel blessed in your life? Do you enjoy good health with family and friends? Do you think you're a lucky person? This house also governs unexpected bonuses, windfalls, lucky breaks, etc. If you feel less than blessed right now look at the fourth house and make a few changes to wake up your luck factor.

Fourth house enhancements

The colour palette for this house is grass green through to hint of apple including lime and mint and all the glorious spring greens in-between. Upward-growing plants are a great symbol for the fourth house, which is why twisted bamboo has become so popular. Avoid tall, spiky palms as we want smooth-flowing chi rather than attacking chi. The money plant works because of the shape of its round, coin-like leaves. One of my favourite fourth house enhancements is the four-leaf clover. We all associate with the magic of this symbol; it carries the number of the fourth house as well as the colour green.

Remember water feeds wood, helping it to grow. Tall wooden furniture, preferably light-coloured, works well here. Ideally the fourth house will be well lit and airy to allow the chi to attract prosperity. A bay window or small extension (less than half the width of the room it extends from) in this house gives a boost to the available luck chi.

Specific placements to avoid in the fourth house

This is a wood house so avoid excessive metal chi in the form of gold or silver decor, arches or curves in the architectural style for the same reasons as the third house. Similarly, this wood area will suffer from an excess of fire.

For this reason it's not great feng shui to have the fourth house in the kitchen (lots of natural fire chi from the stove) – you'll find money 'burns a hole in your pocket'.

Most plants are very beneficial for this area though it's best to avoid too many downward-growing plants such as spider plants as these can have a subtly depressive effect. Lots of beams or downward-slanting ceilings can cause difficulty in attracting the right opportunities for wealth and cause those that exist to flounder under pressure. A toilet or bathroom in the wealth area can drain energy and needs to be remedied by keeping the door closed, the toilet lid down when not in use and adding earth to soak up the draining water and wood to enhance the wealth and drain the energy of the leaking water. You could use terracotta tiles, natural crystals, smooth beach rocks or a statue for this purpose.

Fifth house: Health (5)

This is the central house – the hub that makes the wheel turn. We need good health to enable all the other areas of our lives to flourish.

Fifth house enhancements

There is one cardinal rule for the fifth house – keep it clear! This is your health we're talking about; without good health none of the other houses will flourish. Our physical health needs fresh air, stimulation, natural foods and exercise to flourish. Similarly the fifth house of our homes needs the chi to circulate freely, unobstructed, in order to nourish us deeply. We can enhance this chi further by placing healthy, round-leaved plants or fresh flowers (ensuring we change the water regularly) in this area. The colour palette to get this area singing is sunshine yellow, through the orange spectrum all the way to primrose.

If there is furniture in this area make sure it is square and low, bringing in the earth element. For similar reasons natural crystals work in the fifth house. Amethyst is the traditional stone of healing, but others will work equally well in terms of adding high vibrational energy to this area.

Pictures of ripening cornfields or sunrises, bountiful horns of plenty, cornucopias and sun ornaments all work to enhance the fifth house.

Specific placements to avoid in the fifth house

Unfortunately, many houses in the West don't have the luxury of a clear centre. Too often the centre of the home houses the moving chi of the staircase and the stagnant chi of a junk room or a lavatory underneath. If you have this placement do what you can to enhance the area by using the following advice to minimize the feng shui downside and so ensuring good health is maintained.

Keeping the under-stairs cupboard as a neat and tidy storage area that is regularly cleaned out keeps the chi happy. If the under-stairs does house a toilet then paint it in one of the earth element colours and add some sunrise energy. Avoid sunsets in this area. Most of us have far more photos of sunsets than we ever do of sunrises but think about the energy it represents. Sunrise is the promise of a new day, renewed life force, yang, whilst the sunset is the symbol of the dying day, yin – not the chi energy we want in our vibrant health area.

Remove any signs of bad health, such as overflowing ashtrays, bowls of sweets, crisps, even the TV. We all know too many hours spent lolling on the sofa watching the screen is not conducive to good health. Because the wood element controls the earth element avoid green colours and wooden furniture. Busy carpets in this area can disrupt the smoothness of the chi, as can loud patterned wallpapers and too much furniture. Remember the cardinal rule for the fifth house and discard, discard, discard – pick each item up and ask yourself one question, 'Does this object make my heart sing?' If not, let it go.

Sixth house: Helpful friends/travel (6)

This house governs cash flow, friends, travel and philanthropy. If you found yourself in an emergency at 3 a.m. who would you call? Is there someone to call? Do you integrate within your local community? Do you consider yourself to be a good friend? What steps are you personally taking to create your little bit of heaven on earth?

Sixth house enhancements

This is the house of metal. We can enhance this area using any of the metal finishes such as silver, gold, bronze, copper, tin, stainless steel in our choice of frames or cupboard handles or ornaments for example. If you incorporate oval, round, arched or elliptical shapes into your choice of metal enhancements, it will maximize the beneficial chi. White is also the colour of metal and will work well in the sixth house.

Architectural curves and arches as may be found in a doorframe or window are wonderful additions to this area.

Photographs of friends work well as do pictures or symbols of angels and so on – after all, we all need friends in higher places and this is the house of heaven. A clock with a pendulum placed here can enhance your travel luck and help from mentors, friends and neighbours.

Bringing in strong earth will help feed the metal of the sixth house. You can do this by adding some earthy colours – terracotta, yellow, peach etc. – or adding some low, solid furniture. One of the best cures is to find a round metal bowl – a singing bowl is perfect. Keep it in the sixth house and when you empty your purse or pockets transfer your loose change to this bowl. When it is full give it to the charity of your choice and begin again.

There are many reasons why this cure works. It is a round, metal bowl, which is the shape and element associated with this house, as are the coins, thereby doubling the effect. This is also the house of philanthropy and helpful friends and there are many spiritual ideologies that advocate the practice of tithing – giving away 10 per cent of earnings to help others. This cure taps into supporting that energy by keeping the flow to charity gentle and steady. As a result you'll find that your general day-to-day cash flow improves. There's a bit more money in your purse or wallet. Your bank account looks healthier. You find ways to save money or reduce your costs.

The old feng shui superstition of putting a round mirror under your cash box or till or even paying-in books to double your income is another sixth house remedy. Make sure you don't mirror your chequebooks, causing you to double your outgoings!

Specific placements to avoid in the sixth house

Avoid an over-exuberance of watery associations and blue/black colours because water drains metal's energy. Fire melts metal and candles are best avoided, as is too much red in the decor, open fireplaces, heaters, boilers or any other energy-producing item. Watch out for a predominance of sharp-angled ornaments or furniture – metal prefers smooth, uniform curves and roundness.

Seventh house: Creativity/children (7)

This is the area of children; predominantly our own but it also includes godchildren, nieces and nephews, cousins and so on. It also governs creativity – making a baby is pretty high on the creative achievement scale! If you feel blocked creatively, your projects seem to go nowhere or you have been fostering a difficult relationship with your own children or have had trouble conceiving, then this is the house to work on.

Making changes in this area comes with a caution. If you are not looking to get pregnant and you are of childbearing ability then please take extra contraceptive precautions. If you enhance this area your chances of falling pregnant will increase. I have many clients that have sought advice because of problems conceiving. Barring genuine medical conditions, issues in the seventh house and geopathic stress problems (see Chapter 10) are the main culprits. It's surprising what can happen when you resolve those issues – a few more happy parents in the world for a start.

Seventh house enhancements

This is the second metal house, therefore the metal colours, shapes, cures and enhancements mentioned in the sixth house above will all apply equally well here with the exception of the bowl of coins. A round, white vase of white flowers enhances this area, lending focus and clarity to creative projects. As it is the area of lake, a painting or photograph of a healthy-looking lake works wonders – creativity lives in still waters. This is the perfect house to place photos and pictures of your children, as well as cherished artworks either theirs or yours.

Case study

On checking the house of one family wanting a child, I discovered their nursery in the seventh house. They were still waiting to conceive and in the meantime this room had become a junk room, gathering all those items that couldn't be housed elsewhere and layering them on top of the nursery decor. The result felt and looked like an abandoned and unwanted project rather than the expectant home of a cherished new addition to the family.

I've had many discussions with women on the issue of not getting excited about conceiving in case it doesn't happen. If they prepare for the loss in advance then the disappointment will not be so great when it comes, they argue. I've also helped women as they proceeded down the IVF route quoting me statistics that are never in their favour. I can see where they're coming from but from my perspective, statistics are irrelevant – you'll either be pregnant or you won't. And why grieve for something before you've even tried? Doing that, you never really give yourself 100 per cent permission to go for it. If it doesn't work out then that is the time to grieve, not beforehand when the possibility of success still exists.

This mind-set probably applies to all creative endeavours, not just conceiving children. Often in life we give up before we've even started. Or we drown our enthusiasm with self-doubt and the delusion that we are saving ourselves from future disappointment by being realistic today. This attitude hampers our potential. Give yourself permission to go for your dreams.

Placements to avoid in the seventh house

Fire and water, as we learnt in relationship to the sixth house above, are the elements to avoid overindulging in. Similarly sharp angles are best avoided. The sixth and seventh houses like to let the chi flow smoothly across their shiny surfaces.

Eighth house: Self-development (8)

This house governs all forms of personal development: it is the house of knowing yourself. Meditation, studying, learning new skills are all housed here. We need to practise stillness to know ourselves truly, whether that's in meditation, reflection, contemplation, visualization or any practice that gives access to that small quiet voice within us. The eighth house energies support that quest.

Eighth house enhancements

The element of earth governs this house and a picture of a mountain or mountain range makes an excellent enhancement, especially if it is one you have a personal connection with or have visited. Statues or other representations of your higher beliefs work well, a stone statue of the Buddha for example. The colour palette is purple, aubergine, maroon, mauve and lilac earth tones – think Scottish Highlands. This is an area that is enhanced by cultivating the quality of stillness – perhaps creating a space for your books and a quiet reading area, somewhere to meditate, do your journalling or a space where you can listen quietly to uplifting or inspirational music.

Placements to avoid in the eighth house

The rule for this house is less is definitely more. If the area is full of junk or overstuffed, it will stop you being able to see the wood for the trees and it will be difficult for you to cultivate peace of mind. Wood destroys earth meaning it is best to avoid an excess of wood in this house. For the same reason avoid vibrant, flowering plants, clashing patterns and bright colours.

Ninth house: Fame/reputation (9)

This house governs our status. It is less about being or becoming famous and more about being recognized and respected for the work we do well. It is being known for being an expert in our field and attracting the right opportunities to enhance our businesses, career, etc.

Ninth house enhancements

Governed by the element of fire, increasing this energy can be achieved by adding red, purple and pink colours. Diamond, triangle and star shapes activate the fire chi well. Candles are undoubtedly one of the best fire element enhancements. I have a wonderful photograph in my ninth house of the Dalai Llama's prayer room lit by thousands of candles. Use a red candle in this area to maximize the beneficial effect.

This is also the house in which to place your vision boards, symbols of what you wish to achieve and personal treasure maps. Wood feeds fire and you can fuel the flames by adding wood in terms of the colour green, trees or upward-growing plants.

Placements to avoid in the ninth house

Water puts out fire therefore water features are best avoided. Earth drains fire so be wary of an excess of earth in the ninth house. The fire element always comes with a word of caution. It is fiery chi and can get out of control, so aim for the comfort of a roaring fire after a cold winter's walk rather than a bordello or raging forest tempest in your decor.

It's all about the relationships

Over the years I've come to observe that the houses tend to work in pairs of opposites across the square. It's the yin/yang principle at work. If you find that the feng shui issue is not obvious when you investigate the relative house it may become apparent if you look at the related partner to that house. There are four pairs of opposites to consider:

1. **First house opposite the ninth house:** If we are following our life purpose, doing the work we were born to do, then we tend to attract the right recognition and remuneration naturally.

2. **Second house opposite the eighth house:** Until we know who we truly are as an individual it is difficult to attract a healthy relationship. We need to cultivate our inner independence first in order to attract a mutually interdependent and supportive relationship. Without a healthy relationship with self we can fall into the trap of co-dependent relationships with others.

3. **Third house opposite the seventh house:** If we haven't healed the relationships within our own family dynamics, we are in danger of passing these on to our children in some form. For example the abandoned child may become an overprotective mother. Or the abused child the abuser to his or her own children.

4. **Fourth house opposite the sixth house:** In order to feel blessed and lucky in life, we have to reciprocate by being a helpful friend to others. In spiritual circles we are often taught that the more we give the more we receive. But this is not the whole picture – the more we receive the more we have to give. Many of us are excellent at the giving part but not so great when it comes to receiving those blessings in return. Think how much more you'll have to give when you do!

We're almost ready to implement the changes you've been planning. But first we have to address feng shui 101 – the clutter monster. The next chapter is devoted to the topic because it's a biggie. Applying feng shui without clearing the clutter is like putting clean clothes on a dirty body. Brace yourselves, it's got to be done and once you get started you might discover it has the power to create some pretty impressive miracles without a feng shui finger being lifted.

SUMMARY

- Check your top three priority areas for change resulting from the life-balance questionnaire (*see Chapter 3, page 51*).

- Locate these areas in your home using the bagua as your guide.

- Assess each area with fresh eyes. Can you see the relationship between this area in your home and the area that is problematic in your life? For example, if you are struggling to find a job, check the first house (career/life path) and you may discover the door sticks or it falls in a damp, neglected corner of your home.

- Check the opposite house of each area you're working on to see if an obvious problem is also occurring there.

- Use the relevant advice given in the nine houses to plan your feng shui enhancements and placements.

- Implement these changes slowly and only after following the advice in Chapter 5, observing what changes take place as a result.

Part II

THE PSYCHOLOGY OF CLUTTER AND SPACE CLEARING

'Out of clutter, find simplicity.'
ALBERT EINSTEIN

Clutter, Clutter, Everywhere...

'Have nothing in your house that you do not know to be useful or believe to be beautiful.'
WILLIAM MORRIS

For me, this is THE most important section in the book. Clearing clutter produces magic fast, as it shakes off the cobwebs of stagnant sha chi. Understand this underlying principle of feng shui and you'll be grabbing for those bin liners with enthusiasm. Good feng shui starts with clutter clearing. Stagnant clutter chi can have a detrimental affect on our lives. We need to shift this first, encouraging the beneficial chi to flow, before making adjustments, enhancements and improvements.

Often, getting rid of things is enough to create positive miracles of transformation. Remember, nothing ever goes one way – our homes reflect us. Tidy home, tidy mind. Cluttered home, cluttered mind. It's that simple. Yet, not so easy to deal with because clutter is E-Motional – old emotions get stuck and produce clutter. Our emotions flow through the waterways of our bodies. If we observe a free-flowing, healthy river we can see its progressive, nourishing chi keeping things changing and in motion. Yet if this same river gets blocked, we see how quickly the rubbish and debris of the river starts to accumulate in those stagnant pools and river recesses, which then cause a bigger issue as time goes on. When we understand the hold clutter has on us, we are able to let it go.

Be gentle with yourself during this process. Letting go can be like peeling layers off an onion: we begin with the easy outside layers and then revisit areas over time as eventually we begin to let go more and more. We hold on to things when we don't feel safe at some primal level. Although, seemingly counterintuitive it is a form of control – control through chaos, and stems from insecurity. While clearing clutter it is helpful to remind yourself constantly that it is safe to let go.

Case study

I was helping my mum clear her house recently. She was finding it really difficult to let go of anything and she was choosing to keep stuff that most of us would have happily thrown away! I talked to her about her feelings, asking her what emotion she was experiencing or story she was telling herself. Eventually, she confessed that when she retired, she panicked. Thinking she had no money coming in she began to go to jumble sales picking up stuff to sell on at car boot sales. Eventually the car boot sales petered out but the collecting didn't and now she was living with the results of her hoarding. Having had this realization of why she held on to things she was suddenly able to let go of far more.

What is clutter?

Metaphysically speaking, clutter is simply 'stuck energy' with far-reaching effects – physically, emotionally, mentally and spiritually. Your life will feel stuck or chaotic at some level, if you live surrounded by physical clutter.

The nourishing chi that enters through the front door will struggle to move smoothly through your home if it encounters piles of junk stored in the hall, hidden behind doors or sofas, or crowding surfaces in children's bedrooms, the kitchen or bathroom. The slow, sluggish energy this creates has a correspondingly negative effect on us. It can make us feel confused, blocked, lethargic, depressed and reluctant to progress or move on in any area of our lives.

Clutter also attracts clutter. You see this in the street – most people wouldn't dream of throwing litter on the floor but they will add it to an existing pile – even if this pile is not in a designated bin. The same can happen in our homes: those piles of clutter don't appear by magic – someone put them there. De-cluttering can be scary and simultaneously very refreshing.

Case study
I was coaching Rachel Elnaugh, of Dragon Den's fame recently. She took on a nine-day clutter challenge to clear the garages under the heart of her home, finally finding the courage to let go of the boxes of painful business memories from the end of her Red Letter days. This culminated in a bonfire to transform the last of that old stagnant chi. As the past burned away a

Red Letter Day hot air balloon came into sight and flew overhead – great confirmation from the universe that the work had been well done. During the process she also uncovered some genuine treasure in the form of some long-forgotten, valuable jewellery.

Everything we own is energetically attached to us. The things we love are like golden gossamer threads. Conversely, clutter is like dragging round a ball and chain. Look around your home. How many balls and chains are you dragging behind you? How weighed down are you feeling?

Clear your clutter and life will start to move. Living with junk and mess makes us feel tired and slows us down. Clearing it lifts our mind, body and spirit, increases our energy and vitality, and leaves us free to enjoy life. You know that feeling when you finally get round to having a clear-out – it's good isn't it? Light, fresh and clean. You can sense the pregnancy of new possibilities in the spaciousness; the same feeling the tradition of spring cleaning gives us, as it banishes the stagnant, winter cobwebs. Wouldn't it be wonderful to have that feeling every day?

Look at your possessions with fresh eyes and ask yourself if each object reflects your love for yourself and your home. If not, let them go. By removing the old you create fresh space for new opportunities to appear and by focusing your intention on what you DO want your clarity of purpose will emerge.

Feng shui key

Intention is key to clearing clutter in a magical way.

If you weed a garden and leave the beds empty then the weeds return stronger than before. But if you weed a garden and plant it with gorgeous plants and flowers the weeds have no room to return. Exactly the same approach should be taken with clutter. Nature abhors a vacuum and will find something to fill it. Make sure you know what you want to fill your newly created space with, be it more joy, more love, more energy or more prosperity. This way you stop the old clutter returning.

Getting started

Using the bagua, look at where your clutter 'hot spots' are and how they relate to that area of your life. For example, you might be having problems with money and general bad luck but when you look at your wealth/blessings area find that it's being used as a junk room. Clear it out and watch how your luck and wealth magically transforms!

Feng shui tip

If you moved house tomorrow and could fill more than a couple of bin liners with rubbish then there's clutter clearing to do right now!

The psychology of clutter

Clutter is emotional. For us to let go of things easily we need to look at why we've been holding onto them.

Case study

To illustrate let me tell you about a client with a seemingly straightforward home who had a large collection of wicker baskets. When I first asked her about them she simply responded, 'Well, I need them for shopping.'

'What, all of them?' I replied looking up at the 20 or 30 baskets on display.

To begin with this lady couldn't see that there were more baskets there than she could possibly ever use. Her conscious eyes simply couldn't register what her unconscious mind was crying out. Having them brought to her attention initiated a thought process that brought the unconscious message to the surface. It transpired that the baskets were an external symbol of her fear of not being able to provide for her children. As long as there was a basket to pop down to the village for some milk and bread all would be well. This she realized had stemmed from a period when she had her first child and her husband had been unable to provide for the family due to illness.

From this new place of understanding, she was able to let go of that old fear that was no longer serving her in the new era of prosperity she was currently enjoying. This process was aided enormously by physically letting the baskets go. There was no longer that physical reminder constantly reinforcing the old fear, allowing a corresponding shift to take place on the inside as the chi changed outside.

Clutter blind spots

We all have them. Those areas that bring up our emotional baggage at the mere thought of dealing with them. Some of the most common are:

Basement	Holding on to your past. Too much attachment. Fear of failure issues.
Attic	Preventing your future from fully manifesting. Fear of success issues.
Photographs	Scared that the good times are over. Holding on to photos suggests to your unconscious that you cannot recreate those, and even happier, memories in the future. Clear out photos of unhappy, past relationships. By keeping them you are telling your unconscious mind that you expect things to end badly.
Books	Holding on to old and outdated knowledge. Fixed, rigid viewpoints. Create space on your bookshelves. Keep heavier books on the lower shelves to prevent feeling overwhelmed by them. Donate to a library where you can revisit them should you wish to.
Clothes	Your identity and image. Wear clothes that are the right size and make you look and feel great about you. Everything else is clutter.
Make-up	Your personal mask to the world. What does your face say about you? Is it fresh and current or old and outdated? Anything older than a year is full of bacteria and not fit for purpose. Get a makeover at a department store. Get the right look and stick to it. All those extras that seemed like a good idea at the time are clutter. Update your look annually.
Unwanted gifts	Fear of being unloved, or feeling guilty if you dare to let something you've been given go even if you don't like it.
Garage	Blocking potential career opportunities as you offer a safe haven in here to the vehicle that drives you through life, but you can't if it's full of clutter.

Our need to hold on to clutter often symbolizes something we have suppressed in ourselves, or are deeply fearful of. Every object in our home carries a vibration, a resonance that speaks to us. Pick up each object and ask yourself:

- Do I really love this object?

- Does it make my heart sing?

- Does it enhance my life?

- Do I use it?

- Do I need it? (Be careful with this one – you don't 'need' a second set of saucepans; you do 'need' your car insurance documents.)

- If I moved tomorrow would I take it with me?

- Is it time to let it go?

Feng shui key

Clutter is everything you don't love, use or absolutely need.

....

Identifying clutter

With clutter, go with your initial feelings because your mind loves to create reasons to keep everything, for example:

- **'This might come in useful one day.'** If you haven't used something for one year – through all of the seasons – then it is highly unlikely you will need it in the future.

- **'I paid good money for this.'** But every time you see it your energy drops as you remember the waste of money because you never use it.

- **'It was a gift.'** Ideally a gift is freely given. To let it go does not diminish the exchange of feeling that the gift symbolized. Your guilt will last for as long as it takes you to forget the object you let go of. But your distress at constantly seeing an item in your space that you simply do not like will always be with you. Do you think the person who gave you the gift would want you to feel bad every day? You can recycle gifts to others friends, neighbours, charity shops – we all have different styles – someone else may love what you don't.

- **'It's still as good as new.'** But if you don't use it or love it then it's clutter. Great, give it away or sell it and let someone else benefit from its newness.

- **'It may be worth money in a few years' time.'** One of my Mum's favourites. During the recent clearing process with her I discovered my entire comic collection from when I was seven! Those comics were worth no more today than they were 40-odd years ago. I did learn something valuable about my own cultural conditioning seeing them again though, so I thank Mum for that and I enjoyed the cathartic burning of them.

- **'I've had it a long time.'** That doesn't mean you love it, use it, or need it though. Check in with yourself, where did the item come from? Do you have a sentimental attachment to it?

- **'It's a souvenir.'** Constantly review them because they keep you in the past.

- **'I inherited it.'** This one can be tricky, especially if the giver has died and you feel guilty that you are dishonouring the person's memory by letting go of whatever it is, even though you don't like it. But look at it energetically. You have taken possession; ownership has been transferred from the giver to the receiver. In receiving the ownership, you are also gifted the freedom to do with the item as you wish. In a similar way to unwanted gifts, once you've let the item go it will leave your field of consciousness pretty swiftly, whereas holding on to it and all the attached emotions continuously affects you.

- **'It just needs fixing.'** Give it a timescale either to fix it or fling it.

- **'It's sure to come back into fashion one day.'** True, but when it does that item you kept will look outdated. While fashion themes return, the details continuously change, just like the chi flow.

- **'It was cheap.'** I've never really understood this one, but I hear it a lot. Perhaps it's the sense of achievement that stems from having procured a hard-won bargain.

And it's definitely clutter if:

- You've never liked it since you got it.

- It's not your size.

- You don't like the colour or style.

- It's broken and obsolete (face up to it).

- You've outgrown it physically, mentally, emotionally or spiritually.

Clutter is also anything that you are fed up with cleaning, that doesn't work and is not going to be repaired, or is a hassle to use. If you hide things in garden sheds, garages, attics and basements your subconscious still knows they are there! We're connected, remember!

Life is constantly changing and evolving and our homes are a reflection of this. We never truly own anything in life, we are simply the caretakers of things for a while and then we must let them move on, allowing the space for newness to emerge.

Exercise: Identifying clutter hotspots

Go through your home room by room, using the following checklists to help you identify your clutter hotspots and priorities for clearing.

Clutter checklist

❖ Junk mail

❖ Old magazines, newspapers, clippings, etc.

❖ Clothes

❖ Shoes

❖ Books

❖ Other people's clutter

❖ Unwanted presents

❖ Old mobile phones, computers, etc.

❖ Broken items

❖ Computer files, old software, etc.

❖ Old crockery and cutlery

❖ Extension cables, remote controls, wires, etc. for kit you no longer have

❖ Photos

❖ Unused kitchen gadgets

❖ Old CDs, videos, DVDs, etc.

- ❖ Furniture
- ❖ Unused machinery
- ❖ Out-of-date food
- ❖ Out-of-date medicine
- ❖ Old make-up and toiletries
- ❖ Bad friends
- ❖ Mental clutter, toxic thoughts, anger, jealousy, guilt, etc.
- ❖ Overdue letters, emails and phone calls
- ❖ Unpaid bills

Where is it?

- ❖ Junk room
- ❖ Basement/cellar
- ❖ Loft
- ❖ Garage
- ❖ Shed
- ❖ Other rooms – which?
- ❖ Behind doors
- ❖ Passageways
- ❖ Cupboards
- ❖ Shelves
- ❖ Bookcases
- ❖ Under beds
- ❖ Hanging on the backs of wardrobes and doors

❖ In wardrobes

❖ Handbags and pockets

❖ Car

❖ Office

❖ Fridge

❖ Food cupboards

❖ Bathroom cabinets

❖ Anywhere else?

Now ask yourself the following questions to help you make a plan to get rid of the clutter.

1. What needs to happen for you to be able to clear the clutter?

2. How long do you think it will take?

3. Can you do it on your own?

4. If not, can you organize the help required?

5. Are you willing to make a commitment to a time and date?

6. Write down your commitment.

7. Share your commitment with a family member or a good friend – someone who will hold you to account and check on your progress.

Decluttering is a two-step process. The first step is to throw away, clear, discard, give away, sell, remove, get rid of everything you no longer love, use or need. Depending on the amount of stuff this could take some time, potentially several months or more. Set yourself a realistic timescale and stick to it.

Clutter is steeped in emotional attachment, and our own resistance to dealing with those emotions keeps us from letting go of stuff. We need to give ourselves a chance to build momentum by starting with the low-hanging fruit – the clutter that has less emotional attachment. For men that may be clothes, for women it may be old ornaments, as clothes for women can be a highly emotive topic.

Feng shui key

Look at your clutter checklist above and choose three categories of items to begin with that you know are less important, less emotional than the others. Something like, clothes, ornaments, old machinery or electrical items for example.

Begin, begin it now!

If you have a lot of stuff I know how hard it is to summon the motivation to get started. You may feel despondent at the thought of the task ahead. Be inspired by the following quotation, attributed to Goethe, although it is doubtful he was the original author. Nevertheless the words are powerful and say it beautifully.

'Until one is committed, there is hesitancy, the chance to draw back. Concerning all acts of initiative (and creation), there is one elementary truth, the ignorance of which kills countless ideas and splendid plans: that the moment one definitely commits oneself, then Providence moves too. All sorts of things occur to help one that would never otherwise have occurred. A whole stream of events issues from the decision, raising in one's favour all manner

*of unforeseen incidents and meetings and material
assistance, which no man could have dreamed would have
come his way. Whatever you can do, or dream you can
do, begin it. Boldness has genius, power, and magic in it.
Begin it now.'*

That's the approach you need – commit to it and begin it now. Once you start it gets easier as the chi starts to flow. If you truly work systematically through all your belongings, throwing away everything you no longer love, use or need, the results will be a lifetime of clutter-free living rather than a five-minute wonder. Not to mention the great boost of energy you'll give yourself from discarding all the heavy baggage you are carrying both metaphysically and physically.

You can start small but it is important that you commit to the whole process upfront. Set yourself an easy target of 20 minutes' clearing a day – build momentum. If you're drowning in stuff you will already feel drained of energy and can feel overwhelmed if you tackle too much at once.

For clutter clearing to be truly effective you have to get down and dirty with your stuff. You need to connect with it, physically take each item in your hands and ask,

- 'Does it make my heart sing?'

- 'Do I love it?'

Remember everything you own is connected to you energetically; it has a chi charge. Does the chi lift when you pick up that T-shirt or does the chi drop? If it drops, it's clutter. Our inner wisdom knows instinctively what we love and what we don't. There's an added bonus to this form of clutter clearing – going through everything at once really hones your decision-making abilities. You get good at knowing what's good for you and what isn't.

Helpful clutter-clearing strategies

Clear a single type of item at once rather than room by room. This may seem counterintuitive and a messy way to clear but until you group all the items together you simply cannot gauge the volume of the items you actually own. A little of something in each room can be deceptive; books for example. If you have a bookcase or a shelf in every room, not until you gather them all in one place do you really see the volume of what you're holding on to.

Do you actually read all those publications that arrive? Cancel outdated subscriptions and catalogues. Start a reference file for relevant articles – ruthlessly edit it each month. Ask yourself, can I get this information easily elsewhere? If the answer is yes, bin it. Post should be dealt with daily. Recycle excess paper.

Multimedia

So much has moved online, is it really necessary for you to hold on to that old video collection? Sift through books, DVDs, CDs and video collections, and only keep those things that you'd still love to watch or listen to AND have a device that you can play them on. Amazon is a great place to sell those unwanted items.

Clothes

A good way to begin is to invite an honest friend round for the evening and ply them with a good bottle of wine while you go through everything in your wardrobe asking the following questions:

- When was the last time I wore this?
- Does it fit?
- Do I look good in it?
- Do I feel good in it?
- Do I love it?
- Does it fit my current or desired lifestyle?
- Does it fit my image of who I am becoming?
- Is it in good condition?
- Does it need to be cleaned, ironed or mended?

When you're going through your wardrobe, pick up every item, touch it, smell it and handle it. Do you love it? Does it make your heart sing?

Feng shui tip

The quickest way to lose weight is only to have clothes in your wardrobe that fit the size you are right now and make you feel good. By fully accepting who you are in this moment the weight magically begins to disappear.

There are many places to recycle or sell your stuff these days but always weigh up the cost/time benefit ratio, i.e.

the effort it will take to list everything on eBay for the few pounds you might make and the mess you'll have to live with in the interim against the energy surge of giving it to charity and having it out of the house now. Trust that nothing ever goes one way so the beneficial chi this creates will inevitably return to you in another form.

A place for everything – organizational strategies

Now the second step – finding a home for everything. When everything has a home, it makes keeping your house clutter-free and tidy virtually effortless.

I have observed over the years of helping clients that something quite extraordinary happens when you really get to grips with clearing clutter. You create a space that is actually the right size for the things you have chosen to keep that you love and use.

Clutter doesn't magically appear. It gets there because we put it there. So observe your habits and work to make them more manageable. Most households accumulate clutter on a daily basis via the post, junk mail, daily newspapers, children's schoolwork, laundry, etc. For a busy family life, these little things can add up to clutter chaos fast. You need to install a system and a daily routine that works.

By simplifying your life you leave time to focus on what is important to you. Living clutter-free gives you more time for dreaming, pursuing long-forgotten passions and new creative adventures, and for living to the full. Do not allow anything into your home that you do not love, use or need, whether it is bought, borrowed or given.

Feng shui key

Everything has a place and everything is in its place. Clutter accumulates when we don't have a place for our things to live.

This may sound strange, but by now you've probably got used to that! However, I believe our homes know where to store things and it is worth asking them. That's what I did when I moved into my current space; I simply unpacked something and asked the house in my mind, 'Where does this go?' It wasn't a conscious process, I didn't analyse the feng shui as I went, I just flowed with the space and what seemed 'right'. There were one or two minor adjustments to be made afterwards to tweak the feng shui chi but that was it. We had people to stay a week after moving in. All of them commented on the fact that the house felt so welcoming and as though I had lived there for years. If in doubt ask your home where something needs to be housed.

Start with the hallway

The door and entrance is considered the mouth and throat of the home in feng shui terms. If this area is cluttered up with junk, your home is basically choking and you will feel depressed or uncomfortable living there. Also first impressions do count. Keeping this area clean and fresh is vital in terms of welcoming opportunities into your life. It also tends to be the dumping ground for hats, coats, shoes, workbags, post, keys, etc. Devise a system and ensure that each member of the household takes responsibility for putting his or her things in their designated space. When you come home, there is a place for your coat, hat, keys and bag.

If there is a porch, keep it immaculate. Install a shoe rack for boots and shoes to keep them tidy and perhaps a recycling box for instant disposal of newspapers and junk mail. Store sports equipment neatly in a shed, a cupboard under the stairs or in the room of the owner. Sweep out and leave the door open for a while to cleanse the area of any stagnant chi.

Misting the atmosphere with lavender essential oil or vanilla (put five or six drops in a plant mister half filled with water) will lift the ambience and leaves a wonderful aroma.

Feng shui key

If a space feels calm and welcoming people will be less inclined to clutter it up.

General Storage

Keep surfaces free of non-essential items by finding a home for everything. Get into the habit of putting items away after use by storing them near where they are used in an organized cupboard or on a tidy shelf (e.g. store vases near where you do the flowers).

Do not stack or cram too many items in one space because items will get damaged and will be left out, as it's too difficult to put them away. Make it easy to find and replace items.

Always store like items with like. This saves overbuying and wasting time hunting for items. One client had 25 bottles of eye cleanser stored in various locations in her bedroom. Because they were all in different, hidden locations she didn't realize how many she had and was always buying more.

The best storage is an appropriate size for what is being stored. Nothing fancy is required. Despite what the advertisers may like to sell you, the best storage solutions are often free. I've found iPhone boxes are great for creating in-drawer organizers for small items such as pens or hair clips, as are shoeboxes and gift boxes. These smaller units are perfect for keeping like with like and preventing drawers from becoming a jumbled mess of miscellaneous items.

Store frequently used items in easily accessible places and less frequently used items in less accessible places. For example, out-of-season clothes can be cleaned and stored in a loft or spare bedroom wardrobe, although you may find after a few seasons that those less frequently used items have become never used and can be designated as clutter and discarded.

The paperwork monster

Despite the paper-free promise of the information age, paper remains one of the biggest sources of clutter. Be ruthless with filing. According to Declan Treacy in his book *Clear Your Desk!*, 80 per cent of what we file is never looked at again! Bin junk mail immediately. Better yet take steps to prevent its arrival. Put up a 'no junk mail' sign for the postie and remove yourself from junk mail registers.

There are only four things to do with a piece of paper. Do the appropriate one with each item as it arrives:

1. Bin it.

2. File it.

3. Act on it.

4. Pass it on.

My top tip for sorting out paperwork is to set up a 31-day tickler file. This is a concertina file with enough slots for each day of a 31-day month. Bills are prepared on arrival and put into the relevant day for payment. Same with invitations, birthday cards, directions for events and so on. For those items running into the following month simply file at the back until the new month starts.

Multimedia
Arrange items according to category and then put in alphabetical order by artist or author name. Always replace items you've used in their correct casings.

Wardrobes
Organize clothing by type – all dresses, shirts, skirts, trousers, etc. together. This allows you to see that you own 10 pairs of identical black trousers. Colour coding is optional. This works for some people but not all. Some might prefer work clothes and casual clothes grouped together. If you start with short objects at one end and graduate towards longer items at the other end, under the short items you will create space for shoe storage. Store

shoes in either clear plastic boxes or normal shoeboxes with a digital/Polaroid photo of the contents stapled to the outside. This saves hours of shoe hunting!

Feng shui tip

Utilize regular five-minute bursts of energy for tidying up and putting things away – lots can be achieved in a short space of time. Just imagine you have visitors coming round.

Clutter-free nirvana

Reducing your desire for more goes a long way towards preventing clutter coming into your life. Use the following shopping tips to help you.

- For what purpose am I buying this?

- Hand on solar plexus – does this lift my energy?

- When you see something you want ask yourself: 'Do I really love it?' Then, 'Do I have somewhere for this to live at home?'

- When you think of something you'd like to buy, have a rule that it needs to go on a list for 30 days. If you still want it then buy it. Usually you won't!

- Work out how much you make per hour – divide your annual income by the number of hours you work in a year. When you know what your hourly rate of work is then before buying an expensive item, you can ask yourself is it worth, for example, 10 hours' work? This works really well on bigger items – like the latest flat-screen TV or designer handbag.

- Change your habits – don't go shopping! Find other things to do. As a society we've come to view shopping or 'retail therapy' as a desirable leisure activity. Yet does it really make you feel good to go browsing for things you can't really afford and then have to find somewhere to store them? We can all live with less and we all need to start learning to live with less, if our great grandchildren are to inherit an Earth worth inhabiting.

Don't underestimate the value of clutter clearing. It is THE prerequisite of good feng shui. If you want to feel the life-giving benefits of healthy, zinging chi swirling round your home then clear the pathway for it.

Now the way is clear we're going to take our clutter clearing to a deeper level and in the next chapter we'll look at the feng shui art of Space Clearing – a practice that deeply cleanses our homes on an energetic level. Doing this creates a special bond between our homes and ourselves and creates a sacred sanctuary in which we can nurture into being our deepest desires and dreams.

THE 10 FENG SHUI COMMANDMENTS FOR A CLUTTER-FREE LIFE

1. Throw away, throw away, throw away – know it is safe to let go.

2. Pick things up. Does it make your heart sing? Do you love it?

3. Keep things you love in accordance with the size of your space.

4. Everything in its place and a place for everything.

5. Store things close to where you use them.

6. Store like with like.

7. Don't hide things in endless storage units.

8. Don't overstock items; buy as you need something.

9. Become habitual at putting things away. Don't accept from yourself that you'll put something 'here, just for now'.

10. Don't let it accumulate; throw away, throw away, throw away.

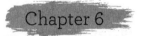

Chapter 6

Creating Space for Miracles

*'If you are able to work in harmony with
the cosmic energies that are around
you, you will feel very empowered.'*

LILLIAN TOO

Until houses are energetically cleared they hang on to their past. The Chinese call this 'predecessor chi'. Literally the fabric of the building absorbs the energy of whatever has taken place in a space. This is why when you walk in after an argument you can 'cut the atmosphere with a knife'. We intuitively feel the tension in the air.

We can see this in evidence with the shop that is always changing ownership, generally because of financial struggle. This is usually due to the site having built up a history of bankruptcy and until this blueprint is cleared history will continue to repeat itself. Chi doesn't disappear, it simply changes form and is absorbed into the fabric of the walls.

When a space is used for a specific purpose, the energy moving around inside leaves an imprint or memory. Over time this invisible pattern builds up in intensity. For example, houses that seem to have happy families where children are born and grow up tend to attract couples who want a family. Similarly homes sold by a divorced couple tend to attract a long line of divorcees, as history repeats itself because of the psychic residue of the events that have taken place there. We can feel this energetic resonance when we walk into a holy place, a temple or church, for example. We don't have to be religious to feel the presence of sacred quietude created by the history of prayer and ritual that has taken place there.

Houses can be cleared of unhelpful blueprints, creating a blank canvas for something new to take place. A space-clearing ceremony does exactly that. It uses a variety of different tools to break up stagnant chi, cleanse memory imprints, move on unhelpful guests and create a safe sanctuary that supports our wellbeing on all levels. Space clearing cleanses and transforms the memory chi in a space and so allows a new history to be created. Energetically it is very similar to colonic irrigation and I often refer to it as 'colonic irrigation for the soul'. We attract houses that reflect precisely where we're at in our lives. If we're no longer resonating with that reflection then we need to change the deeper programming.

Space clearing and purifying the energy of living spaces are practices that have been employed by indigenous cultures since time immemorial. For me, this process is as essential as physically cleaning and tidying our space. You wouldn't want to sleep in somebody else's dirty sheets so why would you want to live in their old energy field?

Our history of house-warming parties stems from this understanding that a house has to adjust to new energies moving in. Inviting your friends and family to celebrate your new home is a way of clearing out the energy of the previous occupants and imprinting energies that are familiar, loving and supportive to you onto the space.

The following are good times to space-clear your home:

- When you move into a new house.

- To bless a newly built house.

- Post-clutter clearing to finesse the chi flow.

- Following any kind of sickness, depression or ill health.

- Following any period of bad luck, accidents or burglary.

- After any kind of violence or bad arguments.

- To let go of a home you are selling – preparing for and calling in the new owners.

- In preparation for a new baby.

- After any major life shift: divorce, bereavement, redundancy, etc.

- If you feel uncomfortable or ill at ease in your home.

- If you know the house has a bad history – divorce, debt, etc. or you know the land has a bad history, battles, disease, landfill sites, plague, etc.

- If you're stuck and need something to get you moving again.

- If you want to boost any particular life area; for example, your health, wealth or relationships.

How to space-clear safely

The following technique can be used for both your home and personal office space. Do not underestimate the power of this work; it needs to be undertaken with respect. I have spent many years working with a variety of traditions, teachers and clients using different space-clearing rituals and the following technique has evolved over time as my personal way of cleansing space. I offer it as a powerful and transformational tool that you can use safely within the guidelines expressed here. However, if you practise on your personal space regularly you may find over time that your higher guidance suggests adding or subtracting certain elements of the ritual or replacing particular tools with something more personal to you. That's great and totally in tune with the natural laws of evolution and the essence of this book, which is about empowering you to trust yourself and your own inner knowing.

Caution

I do not recommend you use this technique to clear other people's space. Space clearing for others is a highly specialized art that requires adequate training. I believe we all have the ability to process and deal with our own stuff but, without the required training, I do not recommend you open yourself up to other people's 'issues', particularly the deeper, toxic energies that can lurk within the fabric of a house. Similarly, if you are in charge of a large organization, call in a professional space clearer like myself to do the work; do not attempt to do it on your own as you are in danger of opening a can of energetic worms.

If this is the first time you've heard of such a process, or you are aware that your home has a history of trauma, then I would also recommend you employ an expert to space-clear your home for you.

Feng shui key

Only use this ceremony to clear your personal space.

Choosing a time for space clearing

Set a date for your space-clearing ceremony. Certain times are better than others: between a new moon and the full moon is helpful for clearing a space ready for new opportunities, projects or relationships; between a full moon and the next new moon is best for ridding a space of particularly negative energy or bad 'predecessor chi', for example if the previous occupant was divorced, sick or went bankrupt. Do not space-clear at night when the chi is at its lowest ebb. Mornings are definitely best, beginning the ceremony before midday.

If you're female do not undertake space clearing during your menstrual cycle. Energetically you are strongly connected to the moon at this time and natural law says that the lesser power always attracts to the higher. Consequently you can attract unnecessarily heavy energy at this time. Shamanic traditions tell us that women are gifted in releasing the pain and suffering of their families. They do this during their monthly menstrual cycle. Similarly it is not recommended that you clear a space if you are feeling ill, recovering from illness or are feeling physically debilitated or energetically under par. If you feel it is essential that the space is cleared to help your recovery it is recommended that you call in a space-clearing expert at these times.

Preparation

As we learnt with clutter, clearing a space creates a hole or vacuum. The first step is to be very clear about the 'why?' of your clearing. What is your intention? If you are clearing out your home because your children have grown up and moved on then your intention may be to ensure the space is filled with creative abundance and reconnection to your personal passions. If you've been struggling to pay the bills perhaps your intent is to increase your prosperity. This IN-TENDING is extremely important. When we tend to our inner voice, we pay attention to what we really want, rather than what we think we want. The ceremony provides a powerful and focused channel for this intention to become manifest.

Take time to focus on your intent. Sit in your space; ground your energy by taking some deep breaths and feeling your connection to the earth beneath you. Connect to your higher wisdom as you contemplate first what you wish to clear from the space and then what you are choosing to bring into the space. Write a list and ensure that the intentions are positive. Language is a powerful tool in the process of manifestation – choose your words carefully. If you make the statement, for example, 'I want more money,' that is exactly what you will get; the experience of 'wanting' more money rather than the money itself. We are co-creators of our life experiences. Activate that creative force by stating 'I choose abundance now' instead.

Be warned, space clearing brings stuff up! It reveals what is hidden. Several clients have discovered their partners were having affairs shortly after a space clearing and one woman discovered her husband had run up huge gambling debts. At the time she was distraught and thought space clearing had ruined her life. But surely it is better to discover the truth sooner rather than later. At this stage she still had a chance to save her family financially. It was a tough time for her but now she is in a far happier place. After a space-clearing it can take up to a year for all the changes you intend to manifest. Often, it happens much faster, but sometimes things have to get worse before they get better.

A few days before the ceremony ensure your home is physically cleared of all clutter and cleaned thoroughly. Ensure food is put away and bins are emptied. This task may seem laborious and unnecessary but approach it with a joyful attitude and your intent in mind and you will start to feel the positive shift in energy even from these early stages of the process. If you space-clear without physically cleaning your space first you can cause unnecessary mayhem, as the cleansing process will magnify what is there, i.e. clutter!

When you engage in the process of clearing with a powerful intent the purging effect can also happen on a physical level. Although rare, it is possible to suffer diarrhoea, vomiting, headache or flu-like symptoms after a particularly powerful clearing. If you've done any kind of detox diet you may have experienced headaches or similar flu-like symptoms. Space clearing is like a detox for your home and the physical effects can be similar as we are so intimately connected with our personal spaces.

It is nature's way of clearing out our internal junk and is perfectly safe. To minimize these side effects drink at least 2–3 litres of water on the day before, during and after the space-clearing and take a 20-minute salt bath after completing the clearing ritual. You may feel excessively tired following the ceremony as your body adjusts to the energetic shift. Harmonize with this by getting an early night. Alternatively some people feel incredibly energized by the process.

Although the majority of people experience an immediate and positive reaction to space clearing, sometimes it can cause a rush of seemingly 'bad' events that can make you doubt the process. It means the ceremony has removed layers of stagnation allowing the deeper issues that need clearing to rise to the surface. These need to resolve themselves before the good vibrations can take effect. Relax and do not become attached to these negative events; they will pass and with hindsight you will understand why things needed to be that way.

Preparing for the space-clearing ritual

I would suggest reading through the entire space-clearing ritual to familiarize yourself with it before you begin. Start by gathering all your tools. You will need:

- A compass

- Natural sea salt

- A shell or a glass of water

- A large feather and a smaller feather

- Candles

- Flowers

- Crystals or rocks of your choice

- An altar cloth

- A drum, rattle, or bell, Tibetan bells or a singing bowl

- Cedarwood incense or a white sage bundle

- Charcoal and an incense burner

- Matches

- A plant spray bottle filled with holy (or lustral) water and flower essences or a few drops of lavender oil, or you can use a commercial space-clearing spray. Bush Flower Essences do one, for example.

- Three bay leaves

- Food and spirit offerings for the ancestors and 'hungry ghosts'

Exercise: Space-clearing ritual

During the entire space-clearing ritual keep your intent clearly in mind. For this reason, it is advisable to read through your intentions once more before you begin. The true power of this process lies in the quality of your prayers and intent. This essence is far more important than the precision of the ritual.

Preparation

Cleanse yourself first by taking a bath or shower. Spend some time getting into a relaxed meditative state through some simple stretches, meditation or deep breathing.

Remove all jewellery and watches, as metal items can absorb the harmful chi you are clearing, and put away all food and drink for the same reason. Turn off your telephone and make sure you will have several undisturbed hours to perform your ceremony. If you have animals they can have a variable reaction. Cats often like to be involved and may follow you round as you work, while dogs tend to run for cover or bark incessantly. Babies and small children (under seven years of age) can be vulnerable to energetic shifts and they are best cared for away from the home whilst you carry out this work.

Set up your altar

Set up your altar on a table in the power spot of the space. This can be the centre of the main room or any space that you feel is 'right' for working from. Spread out the altar cloth and use a compass to find the four cardinal directions. In the south place a rock or crystal to focus your grounding. This should be where you stand to work from, i.e. you have the rock nearest to you on the table. In the north place a feather to represent the spirit world. In the east place a candle to represent the world of the intellect and the mind and in the west place a shell or glass of water to represent the emotional world. In the centre of these four directions place your written intentions as a reminder of your intent throughout the process. Put food and flower offerings in the north to appease the ancestors and spirit world; you can also pour them a glass of alcohol. (After the ritual place the offerings you've used under a tree in the garden or a place of nature. Do not eat them.) Place all the other objects on the altar cloth around the circumference of the central directions.

If I am clearing a house or an office space with many rooms I often make individual offerings for each of the rooms consisting of a plate with some flower petals sprinkled with holy water, an incense stick, and a candle to represent the four elements. But this is entirely optional.

Connect with your guides

Once everything is laid out and the candle and incense are lit spend
a few minutes grounding your energy and doing some deep breathing
techniques. I use the following empowering breath exercise to focus my
energy for the task ahead.

❖ Kneel on the floor sitting on your heels.

❖ Raise your head to the sky and breathe in through the nose, lower
your chin to your chest and breathe out through the mouth. Repeat
three times.

❖ On the fourth breath hold the inhalation, and push the air down into
your belly (sacral chakra area), take three small 'top up breaths' to
ensure your lungs are at maximum capacity, then relax whilst still
holding the breath. When you feel ready release the breath slowly.
Do three rounds of this.

❖ Then take a final deep inhale, hold, focus your intent on empowering
your heart chakra and then exhale whilst imagining the power of that
breath energizing your inner being.

Connect to your guides and spirit helpers and ask for them to assist
you in the ceremony you are about to perform. Every piece of land that
houses a home has a guardian spirit called a Deva that watches over the
space, so ask yours to bless the space. If you are not used to working
with guides ask the four major Archangels to help you. Angels love to
be asked and will always come to your assistance. Archangel Michael is
the protector of the north, Raphael the protector of the west, Uriel the
protector of the east and Gabriel the guardian of the south.

Form a protective ring

Take the natural sea salt and sprinkle a line across all the external
doorways, including French or patio doors, garage doors, if attached to
the house, and the back door. This forms a protective ring of purification

around your home. The salt absorbs the negative energies and toxins that you clear out and is best left in situ overnight before sweeping up and disposing of. Open a window to help the stagnant chi escape.

Unwind negative chi

1. Using the drum, start from the front door and walk round the entire inner circumference of your home in an anticlockwise direction drumming loudly. We move anticlockwise to unwind the negative chi from the space. Make sure you drum into all the corners of the space and under desks and chairs. The deep bass beat of the drum has a perfect vibratory resonance for breaking up dense layers of stagnant, toxic chi. If you don't have a drum, loud clapping, loud rock music or even shouting will do. Finish the circuit at your altar in the south position.

2. Using the rattle next repeat the above process. The rattle has a slightly higher pitch than the drum and is useful for continuing to break up the stagnant vibrations stirred up by the drumbeat.

3. On the third round I use a high-vibration bell made especially for me but you can use a singing bowl or Tibetan chimes. These vibrate on a higher frequency still and are useful for fine-tuning the vibrations stirred up on the previous rounds. You may find there are areas in your home where the chimes strike a discordant note. This is a sign of misaligned chi – keep chiming in the area until they ring clear

4. On the fourth round I use a large feather, which I have smudged beforehand with cedarwood and use only for this purpose. Feathers are fantastic for sensing pockets of stagnant or negative energy that have not been shifted by the drumming, rattle and bell. As you walk round the space 'stroke' the feather from the top to the bottom of the walls in large, slow, sweeping motions. You are not actually touching the wall but are very close to it. When you feel the feather get stuck or sense that it is trying to push through a certain density,

stop and spend a few moments using the feather to sweep the stagnant energy towards the centre of your altar. It doesn't matter if you are in a different room and cannot see the altar; providing you sweep from top to bottom and then towards where the altar would be if you could see it, the process will be effective. Again, finish the circuit at your altar in the south position.

Cleanse the space

Take the incense burner and burn some cedarwood, copal or use a white sage smudge stick and walk round the space again. Use the feather to waft the smoke gently into all the corners and dark spaces of the rooms. Cedarwood, copal and white sage are used by shamanic traditions as powerful purification incenses. The smoke gets into all the nooks and crannies ensuring the space is thoroughly cleansed of its negative and stagnant vibrations. A pot of earth is good for stubbing out smouldering smudge sticks.

Seal the space

Before you go any further wash your hands, close the windows and seal the space. To do this, stand at your altar and imagine a large bubble of white or golden energy completely encasing the space. This bubble should go over the roof and under the ground. For extra protection you can imagine the outer surface of the bubble having a shiny metal surface to deflect any negativity or, as I like to do, call in a circle of angels to protect your home. Congratulations, you are ready to start filling the space with your positive intentions.

Fill the space with positive vibrations

1. Read through your intentions once more then gather up three bay leaves. The bay leaf is from the same plant genus as the sacred coca leaf used in South American shamanic traditions. It is used to carry your prayers to Spirit and fill your space with positive vibrations.

You use three leaves to represent the three worlds: the upper world of Spirit, the lower world of the earth and the middle world of the human that connects heaven and earth. Hold the three leaves together between the thumb and the first finger of your right hand. Then blow your intentions into the leaves. When you feel strongly connected to your positive intentions for the space do another circuit, walking in a clockwise direction this time as you are adding something to the space in these final rounds, blowing your prayers through the leaves into the space as you go. Speak your prayers aloud at this stage. Always use fresh bay leaves for each clearing. The old ones can be dispensed with by burying them in the garden as an offering to Mother Earth or burning them as an offering to Father Heaven. Dispensing of them in this way energetically lets go of your attachment to the outcome of the clearing. Trust that Spirit will answer your prayers for the greatest good of all concerned.

2. As an optional extra you can walk round your space clockwise once more burning some sweet grass. This herb is used to make a space feel like 'home'. It adds the essence of cosiness and homely intent. It is normally sold in a long, woven plait.

3. Finally take the plant spray bottle filled with holy or lustral water and flower essences or lavender oil and walk clockwise round the space spraying into the corners and centre of the room. This 'sets' your intentions and helps take them deep into the fabric of the space. I like to call out or sing general good fortune into the space – health, wealth, happiness, etc. during this round.

4. Thank your guides, spirit helpers, the Deva of your home, the Archangels and any other beings you asked to assist you in your work. It is good to leave the candle to burn out fully on the altar before dismantling your tools. (Never leave a lit candle unattended though; if you have to go out blow the candle out and relight it when you return).

5.   You may like to play your favourite music once a space-clearing has been completed to enhance the positive vibrations felt in your space.

Now your space is humming with fresh, healthy chi, it's time to place the specific feng shui remedies to correct any imbalances in your home.

SUMMARY

- All homes will benefit from space clearing but it is definitely recommended in cases of known negative 'predecessor chi', e.g. divorce, illness or debt and following any run of bad luck or bout of serious illness.

- Set an auspicious date for your space-clearing ritual.

- Only clear your OWN space. Leave other people's spaces to the professionals.

- Space-clear when you feel physically well and strong.

- Physically clean your space first.

- Set a clear intention.

- Perform the ritual remembering that sometimes things get worse before they get better.

- Expect miracles.

Part III

PUTTING IT ALL TOGETHER

'The ache for home lives in all of us, the safe place where we can go as we are and not be questioned.'
MAYA ANGELOU

Chapter 7

Feng Shui Remedies for Disruptive Chi

'Happiness is not a matter of intensity but of balance, order, rhythm and harmony.'

THOMAS MERTON

It is said that a Chinese Mafia boss turns the spout of the teapot to point out who is to be eliminated. It pays dividends to be aware of how we place sharp and dangerous sha chi items in our homes. However, despite the abundance of toads, red ribbons and wind chimes, feng shui cures are not some whacky esoteric idea but have arisen as a means of harmonizing our chi flow. Used correctly a well-placed cure can bring about a seemingly miraculous solution to any pressing problem. They can increase wealth, save relationships, improve health and bring balance back into people's lives. This is the power possible when your chi flows smoothly in a balanced fashion.

I think a better word is remedy rather than cure. Cure suggests a *dis*-ease that needs healing. Here we are using specific placements to remedy disruptive chi flow.

However, I often go into houses and trip over a three-legged toad or hit my head on a wind chime in the hallway or notice endless coins on red string hanging in desperation from doorknobs. For me, this is meaningless feng shui and there's no need to make your home look like a feng shui gift shop.

Case study

One client lived in a very salubrious home on an upmarket estate. Her general decor was expensive with antique Chippendale furniture and cut-glass crystal. She had overlaid this with a thick layer of entirely incongruous traditional feng shui cures. On arriving, you were met by the Chinese bagua mirror hanging proudly on the front door where the brass knocker should have been (and would have been far more effective in warding off negative chi from neighbours). Inside endless red ribbons, crystals and coin cures hung from every offending corner and doorknob. The reason she had hired me? Her life was chaotic and out of control – hardly surprising. We began by removing all these feng shui eyesores – you could feel the house give a palpable sigh of relief as its chi shifted.

Unless you happen to be Chinese, most of us have no cultural reference, or collective unconscious, that can process the meaning of a three-legged toad. In context for a Chinese person it has a history of bringing good luck and wealth, but to a Westerner it's simply something to trip over and collect dust. Far better for us to understand that cures work when they are invested with personal meaning.

Remember an earlier feng shui key, 'If it ain't broke, don't fix it'? Don't place cures just for the sake of it. This is where the life-balance questionnaire (*see page 51*) comes in useful and the most important thing to ask is, 'Is it affecting me?'

The key to using any feng shui remedy is to select something energetically appropriate. To be effective they need to blend in with the decor and your tastes. Someone should be able to walk into your space and immediately feel at home, yet not quite know why. Remember when thinking about remedies to apply the unifying principle – e.g. sharp corners are counteracted by soft, round finishes, cold corners by warm lights. With this principle in mind you can begin to invent your own feng shui solutions.

Feng shui key

Remedies should be 'felt' and not seen.

To place a feng shui remedy correctly, use the following guidelines:

- Clear clutter first. Remember clutter is everything you don't love, use or absolutely need.

- Clean the space, ensuring it is dust- and dirt-free.

- Set the cure with your intent.

- Put the remedy into position.

- Less is more. Prioritize and add one or two choice elements.

Increasing prosperity

Remember true prosperity is not about how much you have in your bank account but about how rich and blessed you feel. To increase our feng shui abundance our homes need to have a place where wealth chi can accumulate. This can be the fourth house of any room within your home. Or it can be the corner that is diagonally opposite any entrance into a room, the living room for example. Wherever you choose, for the beneficial wealth chi to accumulate it needs to be a quiet, protected space, with solid walls and few windows.

Traditional remedy

The favoured Chinese cure is a three-legged toad with a coin in its mouth. Chinese coins on red string and other red and gold Chinese symbols are also used. All of these are likely to clash with your own decor and tastes.

Alternative remedies

One of the best prosperity symbols for Western homes is the four-leaf clover. It has the magic number of the wealth/blessings house represented by its four leaves, also symbolic of the four sacred directions and the four primary elements, earth, fire, air and water. It is the colour green, in alignment with the green, wood energy of the wealth/blessings house. Most importantly, many of us associate four-leaf clovers with being lucky and the fourth house is very much to do with luck. Luck is more generic than wealth and so in alignment with the true energy of this house.

Other alternative prosperity attractors include the image of an oak tree. As the saying goes, 'From tiny acorns mighty oak trees grow'. Oaks are a symbol of longevity and family roots. Another is a money plant – these are better if they are gifted to you (wealth generally comes through an exchange of some kind; either investments, products, services or our time). Ask a friend to buy you one – choose a friend with good wealth chi and it will be passed on along with the plant.

Placing a Tulsi basil (holy basil) plant either side of you front door is an excellent prosperity attractor as is a dash of red (fire, yang, attracting energy). Don't overdo it though, especially if your front entrance falls in the first house (career/life path); a water feature will be helpful here. Alternatively water features can be placed in either the third (ancestors/family) or the fourth (wealth/blessings) houses of the bagua to help the wealthy, wood energy grow.

Marigolds in the second house (relationships) work well as the plant's rich orange and yellow blossoms activate the earth element of this house wonderfully and we need good relationships to generate sustained prosperity.

Back door directly opposite front door

With this design structure the chi comes in the front door and rushes straight out the back. It doesn't have time to circulate and nourish your home with the opportunities and fresh ideas it carries with it. It will be hard to build a sustainable life and thrive in a home like this. To counteract this you need to slow the chi down and encourage it to circulate throughout your home.

Traditional remedy

The favoured cure for this is a wind chime – the sound and ripples it makes as the wind blows disrupts fast-flowing chi and disperses the energy into the space around it. Also the shape of the wind chime with its long tubes works to distract the eye line from the back door. However, the sound can be discordant and irritating to some, they certainly don't square with everyone's style and if you have low ceilings they become something to bang your head on.

Alternative remedies

The principle behind this cure is to break up the chi flow so that it disperses or slows down, giving it time to pause and meander through your home rather than rushing straight through. Here's some example remedies, but now you know the principle feel free to dream up others more suited to your needs.

- Use a tall plant to break up the eye line or, if it's a very long hallway, two or three in a zigzag pattern, along its length.

- A large mirror placed on the wall that the front door opens on to will bounce the chi into the house and slow its passage.

- A bold, colourful, large artwork can do a similar job as a mirror, if it catches the eye and slows down the flow. Sometimes a brightly patterned carpet runner will do the trick, drawing the eye line downwards.

- Dangly lampshades can work, disrupting the chi as it passes across their moving path.

- A semicircular console table if the hallway is wide enough.
- A brightly coloured, wavy line painted the length of the wall.
- Screen off the view of the back door.

Staircase facing the front door

In this situation the chi falls down the stairs and out of the house causing opportunities to fall away with it. Incidentally solid staircases are better than slatted ones because there are no gaps for the chi to escape through.

Traditional remedy

Different books and different teachers will tell you different things. Some suggest having a mirror at the top of the stairs facing downwards to bounce the chi into the rest of the upstairs, while others suggest placing a convex mirror on the back of the front door to deflect the falling chi back into the house. Personally, I prefer the latter remedy as it makes more energetic sense to me. If the issue is chi falling out of the house then it makes sense to create something that will stop and deflect it. This is one of the traditional cures that I do recommend because modern convex mirrors are easy to find and discreet, being approximately 5cm (2in) in diameter. Please do not confuse this cure with using a traditional bagua mirror, which I don't recommend using inside.

Alternative cures

A statue at the foot of the stairs will slow the falling chi by allowing it to pool and eddy around the entrance. If the entrance hall is large enough a semicircular console table with a beautiful plant or flower arrangement will have the same effect. An arresting lampshade in the foyer will arrest the chi too, as will a bright red doormat, especially if it's round. Our unconscious mind screams stop every time we see a round, red symbol due to our associations with red traffic lights and alarms, etc.

Another useful remedy is to create a solid horizontal line of artwork up the stairway, but don't exacerbate the situation by using a traditional falling placement of art following the downward line of the stairs. Instead reverse it by having pictures or symbols of birds flying up the stairs. The iconic ceramic flying ducks heading up your stairwell could well provide the perfect solution!

Front of house facing a sharp angle from another building

In traditional feng shui these sharp angles create what is known as 'poison arrows' or 'cutting sha chi'. It has the effect of 'blocking' opportunities from approaching and the occupants can feel they are constantly under attack or siege. The principle is to use something to deflect the sharp angles away from the home.

Traditional remedy
An eight-sided bagua mirror placed on the front door. These look very Chinese and would certainly be noticeable placed on any Western door. They are also considered a very aggressive cure used for warding off negative neighbours and general bad luck, when a house has been burgled for example. They are placed on an outside wall facing away

from your house towards your neighbour. The idea being that the mirror will reflect back to the neighbour or attacker any bad vibes being sent to you. Never underestimate the power of thoughts – our whole world is created from them and they have both a positive and negative impact depending on their nature. There are less aggressive ways to repel these influences such as the following.

Alternative remedies
A round, shiny brass door handle does a great job deflecting sha chi arrows as do brass letterboxes, number and house nameplates, etc. Alternatively, create a barrier between your home and the sharp angle using a solid gate, fence, plants or hedgerow for example.

Internal sharp corners 'attacking' occupants
Sha chi collects around sharp internal angles, such as those made by square pillars. I used to be sceptical as to whether this level of chi subtlety was really necessary until I visited a friend whose internal walls were all beautifully rounded off. It was exquisite; you could feel the chi flowing happily and smoothly through the space entirely unobstructed.

Traditional remedy
A long red ribbon hung down the line of the sharp corner to deflect the sha chi.

Alternative remedies
For sharp furniture use trailing ivy to soften the edges or a table runner that falls over the edge of the piece softening the corners. If two internal walls meeting are creating the

sharp corner then a tall round-leafed plant placed in front of the sharp edge will lessen the impact immediately. A statue may also work or a flower display on a pedestal table.

Sloping ceilings and lots of dark beams

These design features cause a heavy, downward-pushing energy. If we sleep or sit under them, over time this continually oppressive energy can create issues such as headaches, depression, lack of motivation, low energy and so on. To balance the chi we need to create remedies that lift the energy.

Traditional remedy

A bamboo flute placed on the beam. The bamboo energy of the flute lightens and raises the downward energy of the beam.

Alternative remedies

Paint large, red, upward arrows on the walls underneath the beam and paint over them with your normal paint colour. If the walls are lightly coloured, you may need several layers of paint to completely eradicate the shadow of the red arrows. Uplighters placed under the beams will similarly lift the energy. Artwork can be used to good effect to cure this issue; basically pictures of anything that flies – birds, butterflies, dragons, hot air balloons, aeroplanes, feathers, wings, angels, faeries, etc.

If dark wooden beams cross your bed and you can't change its position, create a light, soft, flowing canopy drape over the top of it. Mosquito netting is very effective in achieving this remedy.

Other feng shui red alerts

To be nourished by the beneficial chi coming into your space, it needs to be able to roam freely. Can you easily move around from one room to the next, unimpeded by furniture blocking your path, especially as you enter each room? If not, move your furniture to harmonize the flow. This means no chairs or sofas blocking the entranceways or storage behind the doors preventing them from opening fully.

Mirrors

There is much written about mirrors and feng shui. They were not used in classical feng shui, other than the ubiquitous bagua mirror, but their use has evolved to solve modern feng shui issues. The basic principle is that mirrors expand and activate chi energy. They are viewed as a water element placement due to their reflective surfaces.

In general avoid mirrored tiles, broken and cracked mirrors because they fragment and dissipate your energy field when you look in them. Similarly, avoid split mirrors on bathroom cabinets. Be mindful when you hang mirrors that there is room for growth above your head. I've visited many homes where the woman has done the placement and every mirror is hung at her optimum height to the detriment of her husband who has the top of his head lopped off in every reflection due to the height differential between them. This can cause headaches (seriously!), confusion and a tendency to feel like a 'headless chicken' when trying to focus.

Avoid an excess of distressed, antique mirrors, as their hazy surfaces don't offer a clear reflection of life. Be wary of what the mirror reflects to, so no rubbish bins, toilets, bathrooms or similarly unhealthy chi including sharp corners. It's far healthier to position them to reflect an image of nature.

Mirror opposite front door

This placement has the effect of energetically pushing people out, although it does depend on proportion. If you have a lengthy hallway then a mirror on the far wall could help to bounce the chi into the house. You want to avoid opening the front door and being immediately confronted with your own larger-than-life image. Instinctively, even if only subtly, we take an energetic step backwards in this situation. This is withdrawing or contracting the chi and such a household will have issues maintaining opportunities and attracting helpful friends. Bearing in mind most people's negative reaction to themselves when they look in a mirror we can see this is not a welcoming placement.

Mirrors placed opposite each other

With this placement the energy simply bounces back and forth between the two mirrors both showing reflected images of infinity. No progress is made because no clarity of purpose can be articulated in this situation. There's always confusion or another possibility to explore.

Street defences

Chi exists not just within your home but also all around your home. The quality of chi that travels towards and passes by your dwelling place is of vital importance in terms of attracting and cultivating opportunities and good health.

T-junctions and fast roads

If your home faces on to an oncoming road (i.e. you sit at the top of a T-junction) you are under attack from the fast moving yang car energy roaring towards your home. To cure this problem use plants, fences and bushes to create a protective barrier between you and the road. It is better feng shui to park your car with the headlights facing away from your property rather than facing towards it. The latter has the effect of attacking the house with the yang energy of the car. If your home is sited on the edge of a busy main road, the chi rushes past and it is hard for the household to grab onto opportunities. In this instance the remedy is to do what you can to encourage the chi into your home, create a meandering path to your front door, for example, or have something beautiful, flowering baskets perhaps, at the entrance to attract the chi in.

Cul-de-sacs and dead-ends

I usually get into trouble for this one because many people live happily in cul-de-sacs. But again let's remember our yin and yang – nothing is all good or all bad. If you're looking for a quiet life and somewhere safe to bring up your children or retire then a cul-de-sac is a good option. If you're younger, active or looking for adventure, you might find the energy of these places stultifying. A cul-de-sac with a horseshoe or circular-shaped turning circle at the end is the best. This allows the chi to slow down, circulate, nourish and still move on, whereas a dead end is exactly that – a full stop for the chi flow. It begins to accumulate and stagnate as it loses its forward velocity. Of course, it does depend to a certain extent on where your house is placed. The worst-affected houses are those at the bottom of the dead end or cul-de-sac. Those on the sides are less affected and those on the entrance corners not significantly at all.

My favourite cure for this issue is to put toy windmills in the garden. They usually come in bright, chi-activating colours and when the wind blows their rotations spin the chi and move it on its way again. Garden centres are a great source of wind-loving garden spirals and fancy windmills these days.

Cacti and spiky plants in small homes

Let's be reasonable; this is not a blanket ban, as many books will tell you. One or two placed where no one is in danger of brushing by and catching themselves inadvertently on their spikes is fine. However, if you have many cacti, particularly if they are placed in the second house (relationships), it can create conflict. Occupants can feel 'attacked'. Cacti normally grow in vast expenses of desert miles from civilization – you need space for these plants and most Western homes have precious little of that.

Dried flowers and potpourri

Ultimately this is dead energy. The flowers have long since had their life force extracted by the air. Use freshly cut, healthy flowers to enliven any environment. Change the water daily as this allows your flowers to stay fresher longer and helps the room atmosphere too. Flowers needn't be hugely expensive; check what you have growing in your garden that you could use for foliage or even blooms, if you're lucky enough. Flowering weeds can make great displays when bunched together in a vase.

Dark corners

As you know from the clutter-clearing chapter (*see page 87*), chi loves to stagnate in corners. It doesn't understand how to navigate those sharp angles. It gets trapped, along with the cobwebs and the dust. A dark corner exacerbates this accumulating effect and means aspects of your life relating to the area where the dark corner falls will remain hidden. Uplighters work well to illuminate such areas but any kind of lighting will help. If you don't have a light socket nearby use a candle, providing it is safe to do so, or a battery-powered light.

Missing areas

If the floor plan of our homes are not perfect rectangles or squares, you'll be harbouring what's termed in feng shui a 'missing area'. Basically this is a part of the bagua that when laid over your home is outside the walls of the home, it may be part of the garden, or your neighbour's property or the street outside or some other configuration. Check which house or houses are missing and ask yourself if the issues related to these houses are a problem for you in your life. If they're not, leave well alone, but if they are you can apply one of the following cures:

- A mirror placed against one of the walls backing on to a missing space will bring in the energy of what's absent.

- A faceted, clear-cut quartz crystal placed in the centre of a window looking out on to the missing space will activate the chi of the missing area bringing energy and focus to it. Clear quartz crystals hung in the centre of any window activate the chi of that area wonderfully.

See the Resources section (*page 228*), to find out where to buy them.

- A painting with a depth of field perspective can create the illusion of moving into the missing space. A tree-lined avenue or path meandering through flower-filled meadows for example.

- Outside lighting reflecting back at the house from the missing corner will illuminate the missing space and give the illusion of squaring it off.

- If the missing area falls in the garden, depending on your garden layout, you may be able to 'square' off the house by creating a decked or paved patio area.

Clocks

Make sure they work and tell the right time. Clocks symbolize progress. Lost time can never be regained. Are you using your time well?

I have consulted at endless houses where clocks have stopped or are broken. On investigation they are stopping right in the bagua house that is causing the client a problem. The issue with stopped clocks often comes when it is an expensive, antique clock that is difficult to get fixed, beautiful to look at and is perhaps an inherited piece. There is no ideal solution to this other than getting it fixed or hoping it is housed in an area where you don't have any issues!

Clocks, when incorporated creatively, can take centre stage in a room. An unusual, oversized clock can be a work of art. But if you're going to use them in this way – they have to work!

Case study
· · · · · · · · · · ·

A home I visited recently had this placement very prominently in the centre of their house (fifth house, health); it looked stunning and was the first thing you noticed on entering the room. But the clock didn't work and, it transpired, hadn't worked for many years. It had also been inherited from a family member who had died in estranged circumstances. Both the occupants in this house were suffering from chronic health conditions.

With the tricky issues dealt with, let's move on to a gentle meander through our homes, room by room.

SUMMARY

- Check your home for any of the issues mentioned in this chapter.

- Look at which areas of the bagua they fall in. Is this one of the issues that came up as a result of the life-balance questionnaire in Chapter 3 (*see page 51*)? Check to see if they also fall in the diagonally opposite house. If you have chosen this area as being one of you top three priorities, take steps to design and place the appropriate cure as instructed.

- If it's not one of your top priorities ask yourself the question, 'Is what this house represents a problem for me?' If, for example, the issue is in your relationship area ask yourself if everything is going well with your current relationships. If the answer is yes, leave well alone, if no, place a cure in alignment with the other feng shui changes you have planned.

Chapter 8

The Feng Shui Trinity – Kitchen, Bedroom, Bathroom

'Therefore the Three Realms are only mind.'
Ma-tsu Tao-I, *The Development of Chinese Zen After the Sixth Patriarch* 54

It's unlikely you have the perfect feng shui layout, just as we don't always have a perfect life with perfect relationships. Life is a constant negotiation between the yin and the yang. Feng shui teaches us the art of mediation, about how to find the win-win for all concerned that enables us to dance with the flow of life. The following feng shui enhancements are designed to boost and maximize the beneficial chi of your home.

Some of us rebel against general maintenance and repetitive household chores. Those of us who live this way tend to take less care of themselves too. Always putting their personal maintenance and daily care last on the list of priorities. Connecting with the caretaking of our homes can be a hugely therapeutic, beneficial and timesaving undertaking. The shift occurs in our attitude. If we approach the job as a chore, another thing to get through, then we tend to resent it, rush round doing the bare minimum, not really engaging with our spaces, viewing them as a nuisance in their ability to attract dust and debris. Such a brilliant metaphor for our own bodies rushing around on a daily basis gathering dust and debris in the form of pollutants, unhealthy foods, not enough exercise or fluids.

Feng shui key

For all its seeming complexity feng shui is primarily a matter of common sense and good energetic and physical hygiene.

When we clean our homes with the awareness that we are engaging and caring for a living Spirit that takes care of us, keeps us warm and safe, and absolutely does its best by us, then the entire process and relationship changes and what was once a mindless chore becomes an entirely pleasurable dialogue with the Spirit of our home.

Harmful sha chi accumulates around negative placements. Bearing this perspective in mind good feng shui is maintained by keeping up to date with the following:

- Vacuum, sweep or mop regularly.

- Repair broken items and complete unfinished DIY projects.

- Wash windows and door panes.

- Remove dust and cobwebs.

- Mow the lawn regularly.

- Trim shrubbery, weed and deadhead flower beds.

- Rake leaves.

- Empty the rubbish regularly.

- Keep up with laundry.

- Repair leaky taps, sinks, etc. – these create a drain on your resources.

- Replace dead light bulbs.

- Replace dead plants and trees.

- Declutter (*see Chapter 5*) – everything has a place and everything in its place – that way five minutes a day tidying keeps your home beautiful and a pleasure to be in, which has a beneficial effect on the endorphins in your body increasing your joy and contentment.

Your home is where the magical and mundane elements of your life come together to create wholeness and integration. Home is where you can begin safely to look within. Feng shui helps us do this, by revealing our metaphors and archetypes – the stories we are dreaming into being – and gives us the chance to change them.

The kitchen, bedroom and bathroom are considered the sacred three in terms of feng shui. If we get the beneficial chi flowing in these areas our lives will function well. We can see how these rooms mirror our own workings. For us to function well we need to feed ourselves with healthy food (kitchen); ensure we get restorative sleep (bedroom); and can purify ourselves and eliminate what no longer serves us (bathroom). The chi enters and also has to leave again.

Kitchen

Kitchens symbolize the heart of the home. They are where we cook and feed ourselves – after all we are what we eat. The ideal feng shui kitchen is a calm, healing space where we feel happy preparing and cooking food. The kitchen feeds us so it is also considered a symbol of prosperity and abundance.

Choose calming colours to aid digestion and avoid red (in both the kitchen and dining room) as it literally fires up energy, resulting in anger, indigestion and unnecessary arguments.

If you have a choice avoid buying a house where you walk straight into the kitchen from the front door. This gives no time for the chi to gather. Visitors and those entering your home will disrupt the nourishing chi of your kitchen. It is OK if there is a partial view, providing the view is of the eating area rather than the oven. Being able to see the oven from the front door is also considered poor feng shui for similar reasons – unknown, external chi disrupts what deeply nourishes us without the chance for the energies to meet and mingle first.

Avoid having the kitchen directly under a bathroom or facing the bathroom door. These two energies of nourishment and elimination are in opposition and do not mix. Similarly it is poor feng shui for a kitchen and bathroom door to face one another. Doors are threshold points and chi flows faster in the spaces guarded by doors. Here you have the 'letting go' chi of the bathroom conflicting with the nourishing chi of the kitchen. The smells associated with bathrooms don't mingle well with kitchen smells either. If we look at the five elements (*see page 34*), we also have the water element of the bathroom conflicting with the fire element of the kitchen.

It will be hard to maintain optimum health and loving communication in a home with these placements. Use the following suggestions to increase the beneficial chi without having to move house or plan a major renovation: the feng shui goal being to create as much separation as possible between the kitchen and the bathroom.

- Always keep the bathroom door closed. Some experts advise a mirror on the back of the bathroom door to reflect the energies away. However, mirrors have powerful energetic effects and, depending on what the mirror is reflecting, this can cause more problems than it solves.

- Ensure your bathroom is kept clean. The more pleasing and uplifting the decor the better.

- Painting the opposing doors or walls contrasting colours will create the effect of defining and separating the two areas.

- Use plants, screens or a bead/bamboo curtain to create a boundary between the areas.

- Create a focal point between the two areas to draw the energies away from the merging and focus the eye on the midpoint instead. To maximize the effect use colours, images and artwork that are symbolically resonant with the area of the bagua this falls in.

Once you understand the principle of creating a divide you can experiment with your own solutions; you may find many more imaginative ways to improve this placement.

Never have your back to the door when cooking as it creates uncertainty and vulnerability. If you have this placement put a mirror near the stove where you can see who is coming in behind you. Similarly it is advisable not to site the cooker under a skylight, as the nourishing food chi will escape through the roof.

Three of the five elements can be very prominent in the kitchen: water, fire and metal, so consider how these relate to each other. For example, if you have a sink next to the stove it is best to have a wooden chopping board between them to feed the fire and drain the water, to prevent the draining energy of your sink putting out the fire chi of your food.

Clear, clean storage in kitchens is vital for cultivating beneficial health chi and it is best to keep knives hidden in drawers rather than on display.

Bedroom

Bedrooms symbolize our most vulnerable and intimate selves. The ideal bedroom is a sanctuary: a safe space to explore your intimate relationships and enjoy good-quality, restorative sleep.

Predominantly neutral, pale colours create a calming, relaxed environment conducive to deep sleep. But for sex, the chi needs perking up a bit so add some passion in terms of accent colours and sensuous textures. Sexy mood lighting can be created with soft bulbs, dimmer switches and candles.

Do not clutter up the bedroom with children's toys or photos of the children, there is plenty of space in the rest of the house for those. This room is best saved for intimate, romantic moments with your partner, and good rest. In the throes of passion you do not need reminding of your difficult labour when you see your baby photos over your shoulder. Believe me, it's not conducive to great sex!

Instead, introduce some erotic, black-and-white art photography of you and your partner. It doesn't have to be all of you, perhaps just your hands or feet or shoulders, a part that you and your partner finds sexy can enhance your relationship.

Feng shui key

Think boudoir rather than bedroom.

Your bed needs to promote relationship harmony. To do this, ensure you have a solid headboard that stretches across the whole bed. This will preferably be made from a natural material, wood, hessian, leather or fabric rather than metal. Matching bedside areas with matching lamps are a prerequisite, if enhancing this house, as is a unifying mattress topper if you have separate single mattresses joined together to make a double. It is good for a couple to have an inspiring view to wake up to – one that you both love. If it has a depth of field perspective (a path through a forest for example) even better as this has the energetic effect of leading you both into the future together. Think about favourite places you have holidayed together or perhaps a place you dream of visiting. It is important that you both wake up to the same view. I have experienced many situations where a client has called me in because their partner has left them and on inspecting the bedroom I have discovered that the person who left had a view of the open door from their side of the bed.

Keep work-related files out of the bedroom. Or domestic-related work – often the bedroom becomes the designated ironing room for many and then the unfinished laundry pile becomes the last scene before retiring. This is not conducive to either passion or a peaceful night's sleep. If you absolutely have to work in the bedroom use a screen to cover up your work once finished for the day. If the last thing we see before sleep is a pile of unfinished jobs and a long 'to-do list' it will create unnecessary stress in our sleeping and dreaming patterns.

Many old homes have beams above the bed. Sleeping underneath a beam is best avoided as it creates a downward energetic pressure while you sleep. One client called me in after he had recently divorced. The marital bed had a large, dark beam literally crossing the centre of the bed vertically, energetically cutting the bed in two. It may not have caused the divorce but nor would it have been energetically conducive to preventing it. Beams can sap our energy, making it harder to feel motivated.

To cure this, move your bed to a new position under an even ceiling. If this is impossible then you can minimize the effect of the beam by following the advice given in Chapter 7 (*see page 140*).

Heavy bookshelves above the bedhead have a similar energetic effect, as do those built-in cupboard arrangements where the bedhead is recessed under the centre cupboards.

There are many feng shui myths to do with mirrors and bedrooms, one being that seeing yourself first thing in the morning shocks your soul. Mirrors expand and activate energy and are best avoided in bedrooms, as we want the energy in here to be calm and conducive to sleep. A mirrored wardrobe, especially facing the bed, is to be avoided. These days there are great, inexpensive solutions to this problem. You can buy frosting sheets cut to the size of the wardrobe doors. Or you can send certain companies your photographs and have them made into a similar self-adhesive film that fits to your door size. This way you can transform a feng shui negative into a positive by using this mirrored surface as a backdrop for your inspirational wake-up view.

Electrical equipment in the bedroom can cause mayhem with our sleep patterns. All of these items omit an electromagnetic frequency that is out of alignment with our natural electromagnetic rhythms, which pulse in tune to the geomagnetic rhythms of the earth (see Chapter 10 for more information on this). Turning the items off is not enough; the current emitting EMFs is still present so you need to unplug the items from the wall. Better still use them elsewhere in the house. The same goes for electric alarm clocks, electric blankets, radios, cassette players, etc.

Falling asleep to the TV or radio is another huge feng shui no-go. We go through a state of hypnotic trance when falling asleep. This phase is very conducive to being programmed; if you have the TV or radio playing you are indiscriminately hypnotizing your unconscious mind with whatever you're listening to!

Clutter in our bedrooms can specifically impact our health ,especially the stuff under our beds. We spend one third of our day in direct contact with where we sleep. During sleep we are deeply relaxed and therefore more absorbent to the heavy energies of clutter. Ideally keep under the bed free or use it to store clean towels and bed linen only. Clearing clutter in your bedroom will support your recovery from an illness.

Feng shui tip

If ill, put a bowl of dry, natural rock salt by your bed at night. This absorbs the toxins you breathe out whilst ill and supports a faster recovery. Change the salt daily and throw away the old salt.

If possible keep the dirty laundry basket somewhere else, perhaps in the bathroom, the hallway or a dressing room (if you have one).

Location, location, location

Bedrooms are best sited towards the back of the house where it tends to be quieter away from busy main roads. Positioned here we will naturally sleep more deeply. We feel vulnerable with a bedroom near the front door. If the bedroom is outside the home, perhaps in an extension, your energy will be outside the house and you will find yourself spending more time away.

If your bedroom is over a garage, it creates an unstable footing and you will be prone to restless, unsatisfying sleep. Besides there is the potential danger of toxic fumes seeping through the floorboards.

Where the bed is positioned in the room is one of the main factors that can affect our energy and quality of sleep. Ideally our feet will not directly face the open door of the bedroom. We feel uncomfortable in this position because our energy system is open. Energetically it can cause a subtle drain of chi overnight and a sense of being 'one foot out of the door' and therefore never fully at home nor fully rested. If you cannot change the bed position you can use a solid barrier at the foot of the bed, either a piece of furniture such as a chest of drawers or a footboard on the bed itself.

Avoid putting the bed behind the door, as you want to be able to see who is coming in. If you have your bed with the head against a window you tend to feel a subtle sense of vulnerability due to the fragile nature of the glass behind you, and the same issues arise with skylights above your bed. If you cannot change the position of the bed ensure your bed has a good solid headboard.

As with many feng shui placements of this nature, one or two nights sleeping in any of these positions is not a problem. It is when the placement is long term that we see the effects of the harmful chi build up, generally presenting as poor sleep leading to deteriorating relationships, lowered immunity, depressive tendencies or some other less than beneficial outcome.

The ideal bed position has a solid wall behind you with a clear, diagonal, view of the door. This is known as the 'power position'.

Bedroom irritants

Check your bedroom for sharp corners pointing at your bed. Be aware of scale. A wardrobe at the other end of the bedroom would not necessarily be seen as threatening, but if it's too close to the bed or you have other square corners from large bedside tables or sideboards, the sharp, square corners of these accelerate the flow of sha chi. The force of this energy rushing towards you can have a negative impact. My clients can testify to the long-term effect of such placements, which have resulted in physical health issues where the projected energy line crosses their body. You can cure the problem easily by draping the sharp corners in trailing plants such as ivy or using cloth covers to soften the edges.

To encourage healthy sleep I recommend using natural bedding. Cotton, silk, linen, hemp, any natural fabrics are great for your bed. Man-made fibres tend to create static electricity, which can interfere with our natural sleep patterns.

'Who's been sleeping in my bed?'

As we discovered in Chapter 6 (*see page 113*), predecessor chi has a significant impact on our lives and with regard to your bedroom it is worth giving some thought to who last slept in your bed besides you. Was it a healthy relationship? Is it ongoing? Did it end painfully? The psychic residue of that person will be in the fabric of the bed itself. If it is healthy then leave well alone. If it's over but still haunting you then clear your bed to reclaim your sleep and open the way for the right relationship to find you.

Treat yourself to some new bed linen at a minimum. If a lot of angst has taken place, for example, you've been through a painful divorce and are still sleeping in the marital bed, seriously consider getting a new bed or at the very least a new mattress. If it is less serious than that take a baseball bat or rolling pin and simply beat the old negative energies out of the mattress. Turn the mattress over and give everything a good shake. This can be therapeutic on many levels depending on the nature of that old relationship!

Exercise: Creating a sanctuary

Look at your bedroom as if for the first time. Does it look and feel like a sanctuary – a place you can relax and luxuriate in, a space that you would be happy to invite your lover or partner into? If not, what can you do to create that energy? Write a list of ideas that spring to mind and commit to implementing them over a certain time period.

Bathroom

Bathrooms get a bad rap in feng shui. I remember back in the early nineties when every tabloid headline seemed to scream the same feng shui message – 'Keep the loo seat down'. Let's dispel the bad bathroom myth once and for all. Yes, we have to be mindful of the draining effects of water. But with a little awareness we can counteract any negative effects with some simple placements.

In addition, when considering the 'rules' of feng shui it is worth bearing in mind its history. This tradition came from an era before sanitation and flushing toilets. From a purely hygienic point of view it would make sense to be mindful of the disease-spreading potential of toilets. Today our world is mercifully different and we have less to fear from our sewage systems.

Every time the loo is flushed or the tap runs we lose a little of our beneficial water chi – this is the draining effect that bathrooms have. Also because lavatories are where we eliminate our body's waste matter they can accumulate lower vibrations. There are areas in our home where this can have a greater impact than others. Ideally avoid a lavatory in your wealth/blessings area, for example, as it drains prosperity, or above the front door draining the beneficial chi of opportunities coming into your home.

The best advice is to be mindful of creating the best bathroom you possibly can. In terms of decor think 'luxury spa'. Recreate that feeling of serenity you experience when you walk into a beautiful spa. How do they do it? Scented candles, aromatherapy oil burner, fresh flowers, beautiful calming artwork and matching fluffy towels. These are all reasonably inexpensive ways to upgrade the look and feel of this room immediately. Make it a place you like spending time in – a beautiful, tranquil sanctuary devoted to self-care.

Include a beautiful mirror that you enjoy looking at yourself in, remembering to say something positive to yourself. Women, in particular, are notoriously bad at this – how often do we catch sight of ourselves and make an internally negative comment, 'God, you look shit' or 'Wow, you're looking old, fat, ugly.' Energetically, nothing ever goes one way – we say something negative then wonder why the shop assistant is rude to us later in the day. Make your bathroom mirror the place where you honour the god or goddess within yourself each and every day. This vibration of self-care that radiates from your updated bathroom will ripple out to the rest of your home and your life.

Fix leaks and dripping taps immediately. I have had endless clients where financial loss was traced back to leaks. Leaks are a sign of emotions not being dealt with, just as tears leak from our body when we're upset.

Case study

One client had been in an unhappy marriage for over 30 years until one day her home could not contain all that repressed emotion any longer and they awoke in the middle of the night to the sound of dripping water. The water tank in the loft had broken and flooded the entire house. Not only this but in the same week the cess pit started to back up, flooded their garden and created a back-flow of sewage into the house. Finally they faced the reality of what could no longer be ignored within their relationship.

If your bathroom is facing the front door, most of the good chi will escape through the bathroom and down the drains, leaving little energy to nourish the house. With this placement implement the following:

- **Always keep the bathroom door closed:** Although this is a general feng shui tip that applies to bathrooms, wherever they are located, it is particularly important to apply when the bathroom door is facing the front door to prevent the beneficial chi escaping.

- **Focus on good feng shui in your main entrance:** See Chapter 9 (*page 167*) for suggestions.

- **Create a strong focal point:** Having a strong focal point close to the main entrance will guide the eye away from the bathroom door and encourage the chi to flow into the house.

- **Energy flows where attention goes:** Locate a wall between the bathroom and the next area of the house and use a big, bold, beautiful painting or artwork to draw attention away from the bathroom. An eye-catching flower display will also work.

If the bathroom is particularly troublesome then add the earth element. Earth controls water. Add beautiful natural crystals such as amethyst or rose quartz or some plants. If there is no natural light, some rounded pebbles or large beach stones placed on the floor near the toilet pedestal will absorb excess water energy. Water feeds wood and in doing so loses some of its own power, therefore adding wooden enhancements to the bathroom will curtail its draining effect.

With just a little feng shui effort you can create your own private sanctuary – a place to release stress, cleanse, purify, pamper, replenish your Spirit and get the right perspective on life.

SUMMARY

- When you strengthen a specific bagua area of your home, the energy of the whole home benefits from it. This applies especially to this sacred trinity of kitchen, bedroom and bathroom. If you leave these areas devoid of feng shui attention you are doing a disservice to your house and, by extension, yourself.

- Check the location of your kitchen, bathroom and bedroom, and correct any harmful chi generators.

- Check the heart of your home – a healthy kitchen supports a healthy you.

- Check your bedroom – a calm, sanctuary supports restorative sleep and loving relationships.

- Check your purification channel – a spa-like bathroom supports a refreshed, vital you.

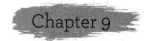

Chapter 9

Room-by-Room Guide to Good Feng Shui

'The home should be the treasure chest of living.'
Le Corbusier

Getting our feng shui holy trinity in order goes a long way to ensuring beneficial chi flow but let's not forget the rest of our home. Everything is energetically connected, so ensuring we have a healthy flow of beneficial chi throughout our space creates the optimum environment in order for us to flourish.

Front entrance and hallway

The direction of the front door is considered of prime importance in traditional feng shui. If you've used the compass directions to align your bagua, use a feng shui colour in tune with the feng shui element of its direction (*see pages 54–55*).

The entrance to your home is called 'the mouth of chi'. It is where luck, opportunities and people enter. If we keep this energy nurtured, strong and active it will do much to counteract negative feng shui design placements or chi draining effects found elsewhere. The front door needs to open inwards to welcome the chi in; if you have a second, internal door it needs to hinge in the same direction to stop the chi becoming confused. Ensure this area is kept meticulously clutter-free. Easier said than done, as entrances are clutter hotspots. Coats, shoes, junk mail, keys, bags, etc. tend to accumulate here. Remember the clutter-clearing tip: a place for everything and everything in its place. This applies particularly to the front hall. If I have five minutes tidying, this is the area I focus on, as it gives the rest of the house the biggest chi boost – we cannot resuscitate our chi if the mouths to our homes are blocked.

Feng shui key

Focus on your entrance chi – first and last.

House names and numbers need to be well defined and clearly visible. Cut back any branches or foliage obscuring your front path and doorway, as you want people, post and opportunities to be able to find you. The best pathway is a meandering one that encourages the chi to swirl gently to your front door. When the front path heads straight to the door it creates an aggressive, fast-moving chi flow.

Hallways are like the arteries and veins of your home. These passageways enable the connection and circulation of chi in your home. To keep the chi moving keep your hallways clear of clutter with doors working well and opening as widely as possible.

Many hallways are rather narrow, which can cause the chi to move too fast. You can place a mirror on a sidewall to expand the space. A side table under the mirror with a letter rack or tray for post and a key holder to store keys also works. You might also want to place fresh flowers here to welcome people in, and install good lighting, the brighter the better, to improve the energy flow.

As you move through your home tune in. Do the arteries of your home need unclogging or is your chi flowing smoothly?

Windows and doors

Chi energy enters and leaves our homes through our doors and windows. For beneficial chi flow, we need to be mindful of this incoming energy. We want our windows gleaming and our doors freely opening wide on to spacious entranceways where we can glide effortlessly from space to space, with a clear view of the path ahead.

Good feng shui in this area requires maintenance:

- Replace broken and cracked windowpanes, these are the eyes of your home.

- Ensure all windows and doors open and close easily, i.e. no stuck locks or swollen frames.

- Paint and repair tatty window frames.

- Repair broken door and window locks.

- Clean windows regularly inside and out.

Remember your home is a reflection of you. Doors represent threshold points, taking you from one space to another, from one state to another. Thresholds are places of power and energy. Each time we move through a doorway our state changes, however subtly. Our energy changes with the feeling of each room. We act differently in the kitchen than we do in the bedroom for example.

Feng shui tells us to avoid doors opposite each other in a corridor. We can see why, too. If two people came out of the doors at the same time they would confront each other at the threshold point of state change – the doorway. Transition states are by nature unsettling and the energy of the encounter between them would create tension. We need time to transition gently between one state and another by creating our homes with spaces between the doors; and clearly delineated doorways.

Take a walk around your home pausing in the doorway of each room. Become aware of what it feels like to pass from one part of your home to another across these threshold points. Is there anything that needs adjusting or moving to assist the smooth flow of transition from one space to another?

Living room

This is where we gather and socialize to do our 'living'. A focal point is required to centre the energy – maybe a fireplace, or huge painting or fancy wallpaper finish on an accent wall or niche. For inspiration look at interior design magazines – interestingly you will never see a TV as a focal point in their layouts. The TV will always try to attract your attention, it is a big, black, ugly box and its feng shui impact is best minimized.

We can do this by placing it in a corner diagonally. This works well to detract attention away from the TV. These days there are plenty of specialist TV and media cabinets that can create a useful storage feature that is also attractive and blends with your decor. Stores such as Ikea have lots of great, inexpensive options.

Ideally the living room will have at least two outside walls connecting it to the chi of the outside world and inviting it in. Avoid using a room nestled deep inside your home, as you will become insular and disconnected from others. The best living rooms allow chi energy to enter the room from outside without being slowed down or allowed to stagnate from moving through too many rooms in order to reach them. This placement ensures that the chi energy is fresh and energetic enlivening social gatherings.

This room needs to be large enough to accommodate all the family plus guests comfortably – think expansive chi. The room's energy is for living and it is beneficial to ensure you have all five elements present, the building blocks of life. Follow the advice given in Chapter 4 (*see page 65*), to ensure you get the balance right for the house/houses your living room falls in.

We use this room for different activities at different times and it can be beneficial to create several areas in your living room that are warm and inviting yet vary in their energetic resonance. An area to sit in your favourite chair with a good book with a reading lamp nearby; this area can also be used for a needlework project, labelling the children's school kit for example, especially if it houses a round occasional table with a cupboard just the right size for a sewing box. Another area will be for getting cosy and watching a good movie and then a larger general area for when family and friends gather. It usually takes time and a bit of experimentation to create these areas in overall harmony with the room. Interior design magazines and websites are good sources of inspiration and ideas. You might also like to consider planning the area in accordance with its element and use these areas to incorporate all five elements into your living space.

Feng shui tip

If you have children and this doubles as their play area ensure you have some attractive storage boxes or a large chest or cupboard in keeping with your decor to store their toys at the end of the day. Tidied away every day, it takes but a minute or two; left to its own devices it can rapidly build into an unholy mess that takes hours to sort out.

While I certainly encourage you to explore feng shui colours, always remember that it is your home you are decorating, and painting it with all the colours of the bagua would create a clashing mess. Ultimately if you absolutely LOVE how you've decorated your room then that feeling will counteract any negative feng shui.

There are also many other ways to bring good feng shui colour into your home without having to redecorate. Using accent colours with furnishings, curtains, ornaments, paintings and so on will create supportive chi. Yellow tones are beneficial for this area – it's a cheerful colour that enlivens a space and is good for gathering.

We want a living room that nourishes and supports our energy; that makes us feel happy and content. This is different for everybody so while feng shui gives lots of great advice it ultimately has to work with what you know supports and nourishes you and your family best. This energy can be expressed through your choice of imagery and furnishings.

Exercise: Connect to nurturing energy

Close your eyes and connect to the energy that nurtures you and see what ideas formulate as to how you can express that essence in your living-room decor. Give yourself permission to create a happy, warm and welcoming room that everyone can enjoy and benefit from.

Living-room seating

Ideally place the sofa against a solid wall with a clear view of the door. This gives support to those living in the house and prevents instability in your family structure. Modern design often places the seating group in the middle of the room without any wall support. Called a 'floating' arrangement from a feng shui perspective this is considered less than beneficial as it makes the occupants feel insecure and unsupported.

Test this principle for yourself. Sit on a couch against the wall and then one set in the middle of the room. Notice how each arrangement makes you feel. Chances are you will feel safe and secure when sitting on the sofa against the wall, while the one set in the middle of the room leaves you feeling slightly vulnerable and uneasy, as though you need to look behind you constantly.

A floating sofa can work if you place a console table or low bookcase directly behind it. Add a heavy lamp or perhaps a plant, large crystal or bowl of rocks collected from holidays to further anchor the chi. Adding a mirror opposite so you can see who enters the room behind you will help you feel protected.

Avoid awkward seating plans. Placements where the chairs are too far apart for easy conversation, or placed with their backs against the wall like a waiting room – these kinds of layout leave large cavernous, empty spaces in the centre, which will be filled with awkward silences and stilted conversation.

Case study

One house I visited had a huge circle of armchairs, maybe 10 or 12, in the living room. Yet a single mother lived there with just her daughter. I asked if she entertained a lot or held regular groups – neither of which she did. I then noticed that I could see the tops of gravestones from the window. I knew the house was next to a church but this room was on the same level as the graves themselves – 6ft below the graveyard height. As a result this woman had unconsciously been providing space for all her Spirit neighbours to come and visit.

There's no magic formula for how close your sitting arrangements should be, although other consultants may tell you differently. For me, it's about creating an intimate arrangement that invites people in but doesn't make them feel uncomfortably close. Furniture should be close but not jammed together. If possible, each seat needs a welcoming surface on which to rest a drink or book.

As a general rule round and oval coffee tables allow energy to circulate more smoothly than square or rectangle ones, which can create cutting corner chi. Overall the room needs a balance of shapes to bring in all the five elements. Lush, green plants make a beneficial addition to any room as they instantly fill a bare, lonely corner with life and vitality.

Beneficial living-room chi is like a piece of classical music – it flows from grand beginnings to gentler melodies and harmonious tones, and ends on a high. When you walk in you first notice the overall harmony or impression of a space; does it all fit together? Then we begin to notice the subtler aspects, the details, the finesse, and the finale is a goodbye check-in on the overall impression – 'Yes, lovely room, like the feel here' or 'I need to get out of here, can't quite put my finger on it but something's not quite right.'

Your goal is to create that 'lovely' room feel by designing a clear pathway for the chi to flow harmoniously from one point of visual interest to another. To help you get a feel for this flow, stand at your entrance and imagine water flowing into the room. Can it flow freely – eddying and swirling around to take in each area? Or is it going to dam up behind some obstacle? Or rush straight out the French doors or large picture windows? Are the doorways clear of obstruction? Are there any poison arrows, sha chi, energetically attacking your seating areas, or the areas where you or your loved ones spend most time?

Artwork

This applies to all rooms, not just those in the living room. Remember the images and symbols we display are constantly talking to our unconscious minds. Avoid anything that depicts sadness, violence or emptiness. A picture of a single woman staring into space will exacerbate any feelings of loneliness. Similarly lots of confusing abstract art that has no focus or direction is best avoided. To increase family luck and harmony place family pictures in metal frames in the sixth house (helpful friends/travel) of your feng shui living room. In addition, research undertaken to find the effect of artwork on hospital patients has revealed that scenes from nature have the most beneficial effect upon our psyches:

> 'Although nature pictures and other emotionally appropriate art elicit positive reactions, there is also evidence that inappropriate art styles or image subject matter can increase stress and worsen other outcomes.'
> ROGER ULRICH ET AL. 'ROLE OF THE PHYSICAL ENVIRONMENT IN THE HOSPITAL OF THE 21ST CENTURY', THE CENTER FOR HEALTH DESIGN, 2004

Dining room

This room has the potential to be a wonderful space for lively conversation and the sharing of good food with family and friends. Sadly in most houses this is often a dead room that only gets used on special occasions such as Christmas and birthdays.

Good feng shui insists you have somewhere in your home to eat together as a family. This nourishing chi cements family ties. If the design layout makes sense, eat in the dining room whenever you can, not just on special occasions. If the layout or the location of the room doesn't lend itself to that consider changing its use – maybe it could become a guest bedroom, home office, children's playroom or library. If you do this create another eating area for the family part of the kitchen, for example, or a conservatory.

Feng shui key

Having a mirror that reflects the food on the dining table expands the nourishing chi, although people with weight issues may need to be wary of this.

Don't place a clock near the dining table. Just as the chi needs to slow down and meander through our homes, we need to slow down when we eat to enable us to benefit fully from the nourishment of the food. Clocks remind us of how fast time is moving and make us feel pressured.

Children's rooms

Children change quickly as they grow and the chi of their rooms needs to change regularly to keep pace with their evolving nature. Engage your children in the design and decor of their rooms. That way they'll engage more fully in the space and are more likely to keep it tidy – particularly if you ensure there is lots of funky storage included in the design. You are likely to be pleasantly surprised too; children intuitively know what works and what they like.

I'm not a great fan of bunk beds, as children need room to grow and expand and bunk beds can be restrictive. If you notice your child always ends up sleeping somewhere other than their bed or moves to a different part of the bed they may be picking up on some negative earth energies (*see page 185*) and their bed may need moving.

If two children share a room ensure each has their own designated area. Children's rooms need a balance between security, bed placed against a solid wall with a clear view of the room, and creativity, a place to house their special treasures, play, daydream and explore who they are.

Home office

Many more of us work from home these days. Use the bagua to identify the wealth/blessings area of your office (top left from the entry door) and make sure it is clutter-free. Keep your waste bin AWAY from this area. Instead, increase your prosperity by placing something beautiful and inspiring here – a crystal vase of fresh flowers, for example, or a beautiful upward-growing, soft-leafed plant.

Ideally, position your desk facing the door so that you can see who enters. This is the command position and puts you in control of the room. If your back is to the entrance, you will feel an unconscious uneasiness, which drains your energy and can lead to feelings of vulnerability and insecurity.

Remember our Form School, armchair position from earlier? The same applies here. Sit with a solid wall behind you rather than an open space, to increase your sense of being supported. If a window or walkway is behind you, reinforce your defences with a bookcase or similar item of furniture or ensure you have a high-backed executive type chair. In front of you, you want space to grow into or an inspiring view to reach towards.

Your chair is the most important item in your office, the uniform you wear every day. NEVER scrimp in this area. It is what connects you to the earth, your personal source of energy. Ideally your legs will be at a 90-degree angle with feet firmly planted on the floor. Use footrests or a cushion, if necessary, to ensure your feet do not swing freely. Have lumbar support and the ability to stretch out. Chairs should have a five-spoke base to ensure balance and solidity, with adjustable height, pelvic tilt and arm rests.

Feng shui key

Avoid placing pictures and artwork above or behind your head. These will distract the focus of your visitors and clients away from you.

Look at your office with fresh eyes. What negative and positive messages are emanating from your choice of art and objects? Are they dull, flat and limiting still-lifes? Sunsets showing a decline of energy? Stark, aggressive metal sculptures? Pictures with abstract and confusing lines? Choose vibrant artworks that inspire you with positivity and energy.

Plants and fresh flowers bring in fresh, vital chi and are excellent in countering the negative electromagnetic fields of office equipment. Plants release oxygen during the day so they are also useful for improving the air quality.

Lighting is important. People are more motivated and healthier when seated near windows and natural light. Dark corners are lifeless and stagnant, requiring twice the effort of the person placed in such a space. Desk or standard lamps are better than overhead lighting, which adds a sense of heaviness and unease to the worker below. For the same reason, it is best not to sit under high shelving so as not to feel overwhelmed by 'things getting on top of you.'

Avoid sharp corners from furniture, shelving, cabinets, etc. Round-edged designs are preferable and they support creativity. A square desk, however, is better for management and finances where logic and decisiveness are paramount.

Beware of too many triangles and diamond shapes, which, in the invisible world of feng shui, represent the element of fire melting metal. An overabundance of fire will create an excess of cash flowing out.

Cultivate stillness. Take one minute out of every hour to just 'be'. Creativity emanates from space. Stillness lies behind all action.

Spare rooms/junk rooms

There is only one cardinal feng shui rule here – don't do it! The temptation is too great. If we have a spare room, within a very short space of time it becomes a junk room, that place where everything we can't think of a place for ends up.

If you feel you need a junk room to store things then frankly you still have some discarding to do and I recommend going back to Chapter 5 and working through it again.

Remember this junk room falls in one of your bagua houses and there is no area of your life that you want to resemble a junk room is there?

Instead transform this gift of a spare room into a magical, useful space. Ask the room how can it best serve you? A room for guests or family to visit? A home office? Therapy room? Or a quiet space for reading and meditation or crafts and projects? The list is endless – use this opportunity to have a room of your own with a defined purpose. This will transform the stagnant chi that gets created in junk rooms or rarely used spaces and will activate that house of the bagua for you.

Garage

This is another area that can become a haven for attracting all our unwanted 'stuff' – that's clutter in my mind and it's clogging up the arteries of your life. The ideal garage houses your car, your pushbike and maybe garden furniture or work tools that are used when needed. It is NOT the place to store all those miscellaneous items that might come in handy – or you're going to sell on eBay – one day. Believe me 'one day' never comes. Deal with it now and liberate that stagnant chi.

Attic

Symbolically attics represent our future. Ideally they should be spacious and empty to give us room to evolve naturally into our future dreams, although they can be used to store items that we use for our passions and pleasures, such as golf clubs, skiing equipment, sailing or diving gear. Often I discover children's toys, endless 'might come in useful one day' items, old school books and other family mementoes stored in the attic. If you are going to hold onto these they are best stored in the basement or in a ground-floor cupboard, as they are to do with your past. But I would also recommend you sort through them and only save those that make your heart sing when you look at them.

Children's toys are mostly never worth keeping unless you are still growing your family and are keeping them for the next child. Mostly we keep the toys for our own needs rather than our child's. We may kid ourselves that our children will want to pass these on to their children when they have them but this rarely, if ever, happens. It is your reluctance to let go of the memories of your child playing with the item and the happy associations it brings. You may think that there is nothing wrong in this and, on one level, there isn't. But it does create chi stagnation and has the effect of holding your child back from evolving and holding you back from evolving as a parent and accepting your child fully as an adult rather than always seeing them as a child.

Another favourite item to be found in lofts is out-of-season clothes. I'm not an advocate of storing out-of-season clothes anywhere other than our daily wardrobe as I have seen how easy it is for them to be entirely forgotten. By the time they are rediscovered they are squashed beyond repair, moth-eaten or out of fashion.

Basement

Similar to attics these are dark, dank places that can became a haven for attracting all those miscellaneous items that we're not quite ready to let go of and yet don't want cluttering up our living space. Which sounds just like the past for most of us, doesn't it? We've moved on but we're still not quite ready to let go of the stories or the emotions associated with the experiences. Clearing your basement can help you let go of the past, releasing those old stagnant stories and emotions.

Garden

Metaphorically gardens are where we cultivate and grow our lives. They can be a wonderful source of renewal and beneficial restful chi for our homes. Depending on our layout and floor plan they can be arranged so as to bring in missing areas (*see page 145*). Basic feng shui in the garden includes keeping the grass mown, the weeds weeded and shrubberies, trees and hedgerows suitably cut back. Just as we would like the projects we are cultivating in our lives to be timely, tidy and structured.

SUMMARY

- Check your general house hygiene; are you up to date?

- Make a list of odd jobs that need attending to and make a plan for dealing with them.

- Do the exercises in this chapter and make feng shui adjustments to your chi flow from what you discover by tuning in.

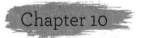

Chapter 10

Feng Shui Nasties: Geopathic Stress and Technostress

'No dwelling shall be built until the earth diviners have confirmed the intended building site to be free of earth demons.'
CHINESE EMPEROR KUANG YU (2205–2197BCE)

Electromagnetic fields and radiation are not new. Since the beginning of time, this planet has been subject to all manner of cosmic and other electromagnetic frequencies and radiation. Issuing from natural phenomena, such as volcanoes, the sun, underground lava flows, subterranean waterways, decaying granite (radon gas), supernova, planets, etc., these frequencies are normal and part of life's great diversity. Some of that energy is good for us (sheng chi) and some detrimental (sha chi). The traditional feng shui masters understood this and took these earth energies into account when assessing a good site for a building. We need to be aware of them to if we are to provide a safe place for ourselves to live.

Today, we are in uncharted territory. It is just over a century since the advent of electricity and it took decades before it became universally available. That is miniscule in terms of human evolution. It takes eons for any species to adapt genetically to changing environmental threats. If we manage to survive as a species then in generations to come we will eventually develop the ability to harmonize these adverse emissions. Mains electricity was introduced in 1882; originally direct current (DC) was the preferred method of delivery but this posed a problem to supply and it was shortly changed to alternative current (AC). As the name implies, this current oscillates to and fro rather than travelling directly. It is the electromagnetic fields generated by this current that are now being recognized as a contributing factor in many modern health issues.

In addition we have the explosion in microwave technology, Wi-Fi, smart phones and so on, which provides a constant pulse of invisible radiation that can travel through bricks and mortar and into our sensitive human bodies with ease. If we look at the development of disease patterns over the last century it has changed dramatically in nature and autoimmune deficiency diseases of which cancer, one of the biggest killers, is growing at an exponential rate. Only time will tell the real impact of our technological and chemical age on our health and wellbeing.

Research shows that pollution inside our homes can be 10 times greater than outside. This pollution comes in all sorts of hidden forms, from air fresheners, household cleaners, toxic paint fumes, outgassing from new synthetic carpets to electromagnetic frequencies (EMFs) and microwave radiation.

Toxic frequencies

This is an enormous field of study with ever more research coming to light, which we can't possibly cover in depth here, however, I have recommended some further reading in the Resources section (*see page 228*) if you'd like to explore this topic further. Meanwhile, we're going to look at the basics of protecting ourselves from harmful toxins.

Some people are far more sensitive to these toxic frequencies than others in exactly the same way some people suffer food allergies and others don't. Location, genetics, upbringing, income all play a part in our overall wellbeing. The good news is there are always things we can do to improve our environment. We also have the power of resilience and the ability to self-heal. However if you do suffer from headaches, irritability, ME, insomnia, excessive nightmares, chronic aches and pains or other health disturbances then it is worth exploring the advice given here.

An EMF is a field of energy created by electrically charged objects. It has two 'components', one magnetic, the other electric. The electric field is produced by stationary charges and the magnetic field by moving charges (currents). You can't see, feel or hear electromagnetic fields, apart from visible light, which is a part of the electromagnetic spectrum.

We have evolved with the natural levels of EMFs produced by both the sun and world around us. However, the earth's magnetic fields are static fields, unlike man-made alternating current (AC), which has no natural counterpart. Microwave frequency is a relatively new phenomenon: 100 years ago the background radiation was millions of times lower than it is now, and it is only since the recent mobile phone boom that the modern, digitally pulsed signals have become ubiquitous in the Western world.

Research has shown that exposure to high EMFs, especially near the head, can interfere with the efficiency of the pineal gland, which releases melatonin and serotonin. In those that are sensitive this can lead to sleep disturbances and depression. With long-term exposure these discordant frequencies lower our immune system, as they are a form of stress. Sources of EMFs in the bedroom include electric blankets, clock radios, TVs, music systems, hairdryers, etc. The problem is exacerbated if you use synthetic bed linen and have a metal bed as this increases the conductive ability of the electric currents.

Exercise: Daily earth energies

Use this ancient shamanic practice to get your daily dose of beneficial earth energies.

Stand with your left palm facing the ground and your right hand resting by your side. Imagine opening the centre of your left palm, soles of feet and perineum as though they were mouths and allow the energy of the earth to soak into you through them, just like a sponge soaking up water.

Do this for five minutes daily or when you feel you need it. Make sure you are standing on a healthy, lush piece of ground to do this!

Digital cordless phones, mobile phones and Wi-Fi all give off microwave emissions. Increasingly research suggests links to loss of memory, headaches, premature ageing and tumours from this type of radiation. A good book that dissects the research is *Disconnect: The Truth About Cell Phone Radiation, What the Industry Has Done to Hide It, and How to Protect Your Family*, by Devra Davis. And for those of you that watch TV in bed or, worse still, fall asleep with it on, the imperceptible flickering of the TV screen creates oscillations that cause abnormal responses in the brain that can bring about headaches, eyestrain and fatigue.

Outgassing from poisons including formaldehyde in new furniture, carpets and some paints combined with sealed double-glazing leads to new homes becoming a toxic incubator. We can wake up with headaches, nausea, flu-like symptoms, allergies, dermatitis and a general feeling of malaise.

Feng shui tip

Always sleep in a well-ventilated room. If you cannot sleep with a window open air the room thoroughly before going to bed.

Geopathic stress

Lastly there is what is known as *geo* (meaning earth) *pathic* (meaning disease) stress. Geopathic stress (GS) occurs when the natural geomagnetic field of the earth becomes distorted. It's the term used for areas of the earth that are stressed out and sick. If we spend long periods of time sleeping or sitting on lines of GS we too can become stressed out and sick if we are sensitive to these energies. This may be entirely new information to you but GS has been extensively researched and documented over the years. Dulwich Health Authority is a good resource for further information. Common signs of GS include:

- chronic clutter

- light bulbs blowing frequently

- electrical items malfunctioning more often than considered normal

- musty, damp smell

- general feeling of unease or discomfort

- plagues of ants or wasps

- ivy and nettles

- unusually twisted trees, normally growing in the direction of the offending stream

- strange gaps in hedgerow growth

- infertile fruit trees

- areas of the garden where plants don't thrive

GS is often discovered at the site of notorious accident black spots, in areas where vandalism is rife and violence and crime flourish. European geomantic traditions refer to these paths of stress as 'black streams'. Traditional feng shui refers to them as lines of underground sha chi or toxic energy. The study of geopathology is growing and now includes the modern phenomena of electromagnetism.

Man-made phenomena such as railway cuttings, quarries, mines, tall buildings with steel pilings, sewers, underground tunnels, drains and buried utility pipes can also disturb the earth's healthy geomagnetic field. Anybody living above these distortions will experience earth stress, which can weaken the immune system leading to further problems if the exposure is long term.

Certain animals are either repelled or attracted by these energies. Cats love them and dogs avoid them. Use common sense though, the cat may sleep on the end of your bed because it's their favourite place to be rather than because it can sense GS! Babies, however, will tend to sleep away from GS and a good indication that there's a problem is when you regularly find your baby curled up in an odd corner of the cot. They actually look like they are trying to get away from something. In terms of our home the main thing we need to know is that we're not sleeping on it, or sitting on it for long periods.

Exercise: Checking for geopathic stress

To check for GS in your home, take an old wire coat hanger. Untwist the hanger part and break or use wire cutters to break the hanger in two. You should have two similar-size halves that you can bend into two 90-degree-angled rods. Walk, slowly from one side of a room to the other and see if the rods react. Now walk slowly the other way and see if the rods react. If the rods cross over or react wildly see where this line is in relation to where you sit or sleep. If it crosses over your bed move it to a position free of any crossing lines. If it crosses your favourite armchair – move the armchair to a more favourable position.

We have a natural affinity with the healthy EMF of the earth, which resonates at 7.83hz – almost identical to human alpha brainwaves. Anything discordant to this will affect our energy field and react via the dowsing rods. (To buy professional dowsing rods see Resources section.)

If the above seems too difficult and you are concerned about the possibility of GS consider employing a professional dowser such as myself or visit www.britishdowsers.org for a list of qualified dowsers.

If you cannot move your bed, there are alternative solutions for GS including a number of plug-in devices such as the Raditech and the Helios. In my experience the Helios is the more effective product (see Resources section). These devices create a protective barrier around your home whilst they are plugged in. They do not actually cure the underlying issue.

The most effective long-term cure is earth acupuncture, which works in exactly the same way as traditional acupuncture except you treat the meridians of the earth with large wooden needles, rather than the body with small metal needles. GS and earth acupuncture have always been integral to feng shui practice. Particular relevance is paid to GS lines that run across the front door (blocking opportunities), the bed (health issues) and the centre of the house causing general bad luck.

If you've recently moved and are experiencing unusually bad luck, financial drains, or disturbed sleep, headaches and increased anxiety and stress levels chances are there's some GS lurking.

What can we do to protect ourselves?

Remember the big issue with all of these frequencies is that they are in opposition to our naturally produced EMFs. It is not that they actually cause physical illness (well, not yet proven definitely) but they subtly stress our system, which over time leads to a lowering of the immune system, which can then lead to more serious conditions.

Amount, strength and length of exposure are pertinent too. We need the beneficial rays of the sun for optimum health. Yet, if we spend too long in the sun we develop sunburn, premature ageing and potentially skin cancer. It's good to bear in mind the life philosophy of my 100-year-old grandmother, 'A little bit of what you fancy does you good, a lot of it never did.' Certainly seems to have worked for her!

We cannot avoid the onslaught of the modern world. Even if you resist Wi-Fi, if your neighbour installs it you'll be affected anyway. If you live in an urban area every time you step outside you are being bombarded with these frequencies. The key is to reduce stress and keep your immune system as healthy as possible. All the things we already know help with this, such as natural, healthy foods, plenty of water, exercise, meditation and so on. We also need good sleep as our immune system is repaired and strengthened during the night. Ensure your home is as supportive as possible by taking action on the advice given below.

Using feng shui to reduce environmental pollution

Invest in house plants. Use peace lilies and spider plants in rooms with electrical equipment, computers, etc. Plants effectively remove formaldehyde, acetone, benzene and a variety of other noxious office emissions. The areca palm removes every single tested toxin including cigarette smoke. Boston ferns regulate humidity and remove formaldehyde. Use orchids in the bedroom as they release oxygen at night rather than during the day. NASA has done the most extensive research into how the earth produces and sustains fresh air, and discovered that houseplants can purify and revitalize the air in sealed chambers.

Place unpolished, clear quartz crystals on fuse boxes, electricity meters and near your computer. These soak up all the pollutants. Be aware they do get 'full' though and will need cleansing regularly by rinsing under the tap in clean running water or burying in dry sea-salt for 24 hours.

- Plug in a Helios device (also great for harmonizing GS; see the Resources section (*page 228*). It's the cheapest, smallest and in my experience the best on the market of these devices; others include the Geomack and the Raditech.

- Plug in an ionizer in rooms containing electrical equipment, to help release more negative ions into the atmosphere to counteract all the positive ions being belched out by the equipment.

- Cheaper than above – get a damp, **not wet**, cloth and wipe over your computer screen and keyboard each morning before using it. It adds negative ions to the atmosphere.

- Place a bowl of sea salt in the office – remember to throw it away after a few days and replace it with a new batch. Salt is great at absorbing environmental pollutants. Please don't use the salt for any culinary purpose afterwards; it will spoil your food.

- Keep your bedroom as electrically silent as possible by unplugging all items near the bed before sleep. For the ultimate in peaceful sleep get your electrician to install a power demand switch for the bedroom circuit. You will need a torch near the bed, as the lights won't work.

- Use a battery or wind-up alarm clock, NEVER your mobile phone. Keep digital handsets and especially base stations a long way from the bedroom; these emit powerful radio signals that can interfere with our healthy electromagnetic energy. Turn off your Wi-Fi and computers at night.

- Use natural fibre bed linen, ideally organic cotton, which allows skin to breathe.

Enhancing wellbeing

Our ability to cope in the world is a reflection of our physical and mental health, which has its foundation in the food we consume. Good living begins in the kitchen, the heart of the home. Unfortunately modern living has turned these nerve centres of health into potentially toxic environments. To reclaim your kitchen as a centre of wellbeing here are some tips for keeping harmful toxins at bay:

- Make a commitment to a healthy you by clearing the kitchen clutter. Look through your food cupboards including the fridge and eradicate all the out-of-date nasties found lurking there. This will allow your kitchen to breathe again, create space and encourage you to fill it with fresh food.

- Eat as much chemical-free, organic fruit and veg as possible. If you're on a tight budget, most harmful pesticides can be removed from non-organic produce by soaking in clean water for 10 minutes with a cupful of cider vinegar added.

- Avoid using the microwave because it can leak higher radiation levels than recommended – Dr Lita Lee's book, *Health Effects of Microwave Radiation – Microwave Ovens*, in particular, makes useful reading as it describes the dangers that microwaves can pose and scrutinizes the available research. If you insist on keeping it minimize its use. Remove all plastic packaging and ideally transfer the food into a ceramic or glass container. This is especially relevant for foods that contain fat. The combination of fat, high heat and plastic releases dioxins, which are highly poisonous to the cells of our bodies. If you stood in front of an operational microwave with no door your insides would cook. Plants watered with microwaved water die. Think what happens when you heat the baby's milk in the microwave.

- Instead of covering dishes with cling film use paper towels. As the food is microwaved the high heat causes poisonous toxins to literally melt out of the plastic wrap and drip into the food. Mmm tasty!

- Don't freeze your plastic bottles with water in, or leave them in the sun, as this releases dioxins from the plastic. Preferably use glass bottles, install a reverse osmosis water system or get a filter jug and stop buying bottled water altogether. You will be doing the planet a great service by consuming a little less plastic.

- Use natural alternatives to chemical cleaners whenever possible. These have been proven to cause conditions from headaches, dermatitis and allergies to asthma. There are plenty of efficient, eco products available these days. Alternatively hot water and a few drops of tea tree oil is a fantastic natural disinfectant. Lemons make great natural bleach and the power of vinegar and newspaper to bring a super shine to glass and mirrors is vastly overlooked. Think of all the money you'll save too!

- Ban the TV from the kitchen. Do you really want all that toxic news filtering into your food? The mood you are in whilst cooking affects the taste and quality of the food prepared. Don't cook when angry or upset. For best results play soothing or uplifting music or listen to something fun or inspiring on the radio. Even better, get the family involved in making meals – cook, chat and eat together.

- Limit your use of tinned, processed and pre-packaged food. All contain chemicals harmful to the body and very little nutritional content. There are many fresh, quick alternatives such as wok-fried veggies; steamed fish; home-made vegetable soups and stews. These are generally cheaper too.

- Take up meditation, tai chi, chi gung, yoga or any other form of stress-relieving activity and make it a daily practice.

- Once or twice a year consider doing a detox. My favourite is an old one, *Lesley Kenton's 10-day Rebalance Programme*. It works, is quite pleasurable and not too extreme. Remember feng shui is all about maintaining a state of homeostasis. If we starve ourselves for weeks, the pendulum will swing wildly and decisively back the other way causing us to overeat and slip back into bad eating habits fast.

Following these simple guidelines will go a long way in helping you build a strong biological defence mechanism and give your immune system the strength to fight invading toxins.

SUMMARY

- Check your neighbourhood. Do you have electricity substations, mobile masts, overhead power lines or pylons close by?

- Are you experiencing any of the health symptoms mentioned in this chapter? If so dowse your home for geopathic stress and take remedial action if necessary.

- Check your bedroom. Do you need to remove electrical items from around the bedhead?

- Check your kitchen. Is it conducive to healthy living?

- How do you de-stress? Do you meditate? Spend time in nature; listen to music; take regular 'me' time; exercise etc.?

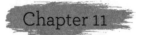
Chapter 11

Buying and Selling
with Feng Shui

*'The journey of a thousand miles
begins with a single step.'*
Lao Tzu

Using the power of feng shui to buy and sell homes really works. My last two homes sold for more than the asking price to the first person that walked through the door – both sales took less than half an hour. The second one sailed through so smoothly it almost convinced the estate agent that maybe there was something to this feng shui business! I was recently asked to help sell a home that had been on the market for some time as the client had found their dream home but couldn't afford a bridging loan. In this instance a space-clearing ceremony and a few small feng shui changes resulted in a buyer the same week and now they are happily living in their idea of heaven.

Things to consider when choosing a home

Buying a home is usually the most expensive undertaking we engage in and yet we probably spend more time choosing a new phone than we do choosing our home. When I recently sold my London flat the buyer viewed it once, for less than 20 minutes. This is quite extraordinary bearing in mind the sum of money he was about to part with. I think this is linked to our indigenous soul that innately understands our relationship with our environment and gives rise to that instant 'knowing' that many of us get when we find the right home.

Case study

I think the most extraordinary example of feng shui's selling power was an incredibly grand house worth several million. During my visit our conversation was interrupted every few seconds by planes zooming overhead. The flight path had changed since my client had brought the property and now the planes were unbearably low and extremely frequent. We literally couldn't hear ourselves speak as they flew over every few minutes. I jokingly remarked that she would need to find a deaf buyer. Certainly this was an issue I couldn't resolve with feng shui; at least I didn't think so until two weeks after my visit she rang to tell me she had sold the house to someone who had only one ear!

I believe homes choose us as much as we choose them. If our homes are truly metaphors of the self, then it makes sense that we will attract a home that resonates with who we are at that moment – consequently when we cross the threshold we recognize ourselves at some level, it feels comfortable and we get a distinct 'yes' inside. That was certainly true for my current home. Although I am only renting, I had been looking for over a year and nothing had shown up. I had been intending to move to the southwest, as I have many friends there and I love the area. However, by a strange series of synchronicities I ended up in the southeast, not an area I am familiar with, yet within days I had found my perfect home. I only saw one room and the garden and immediately 'knew' it was the one – I didn't need to see the rest of the house. Pay attention to these feelings, they are absolutely key to a good purchase. Failing to do so can have dire consequences, as demonstrated by the following story.

Case study

A client purchased a house where a murder had taken place. She did not discover this until after the purchase but I'm not sure it would have altered her decision. I asked her what she had felt on first viewing the house – 'Oh, I absolutely hated it,' she immediately retorted, so I had to ask why she'd bought it! She then proceeded to give me a long explanation of all the reasons that had overridden her own innate sense of knowing – it was cheap, had a large garden, was close to her children's schools, the land could be developed, etc. It all sounds perfectly reasonable and many people would do the same – a good investment opportunity after all. Yet, by the time this client found me she was at her wits' end. Their business had failed; the house they tried to build on the land was plagued by endless problems that had cost them thousands, the children were always sick and their marriage was on the rocks owing to the strain of it all. Since moving to this house they had effectively lost all they had built up and were on the verge of bankruptcy.

Feng shui key

When choosing a new home always favour the truth of your inner 'knowing' over practical considerations.

Discover as much as possible about the history of a home you are considering buying. A home that's being sold because the occupants are growing and need more space will have far greater beneficial chi than a home that is being sold because the owner went bankrupt. Remember what you learnt in Chapter 6 on space clearing – history has a tendency to repeat itself unless the energetic blueprint is removed.

When buying look for a feeling of 'home', a sanctuary that makes your heart sing. A place you want to linger and invite friends to, a place where you can imagine placing your furniture. Tune in to the Spirit of Place to decide if this will be a home that will nurture and nourish you and provide abundant support for your physical, emotional and spiritual self. This inner feng shui is ultimately far more important than whether you live in a model feng shui house. Most houses will have issues of some kind, as they were not originally designed and built with feng shui principles in mind.

Make a list of what your perfect home needs to include. This gives you a head start in recognizing it when you see it. List everything you can think of. The clearer you are, the greater your chances of having it. You can edit this list and send it to estate agents as your buying criteria – this will save a huge amount of repetitive conversations and time wasting as you are sent to yet another viewing that doesn't match your requirements. One word of caution though – we don't always know what is best for us; if something comes on to your radar that doesn't fit your criteria yet just 'feels' right, please do check it out.

Quality of chi

Your first consideration when buying a new home is to assess the quality of chi in the land itself and the chi approaching the property. Does it look and feel vibrant? Is the vegetation lush and healthy, full of life force and vitality? Land that is arid with vegetation struggling to thrive, or full of ivy and stinging nettles, is a sign of stagnant, depleted chi.

Landscape

When choosing a suitable house we need to consider the principles of Form School feng shui, our armchair idea from Chapter 1 (*see page 19*). When viewing a property always check the topographical layout of the four celestial animals:

Turtle

Look at the back of the property. Is there suitable support? Tall, solid structures, a well-built garden fence? These help contain the chi of a home. Avoid homes that back on to active railway lines (destabilizing chi), or where the back garden slopes away downhill (escaping chi). The ideal is to have the land at the back of the house slightly higher than the land at the front.

Phoenix

Standing at the front of the property, look out at the view. This is your future. Avoid overbearing buildings, or anything that seems to be 'attacking' you. Does the view seem spacious, open and pleasant? This can be true even if the property is in a row of terraces; are the homes well kept and maintained, is there a good feel to the street, etc.

Dragon

Look to the right as you stand facing the property. Ideally this side of the house should be slightly taller than the left-hand side. This is the male/yang side, the 'active' side and is the best place for parking cars and placing the dustbins, if you have to have them at the front of the property.

Tiger

Look to the left as you stand facing the front of the property. Ideally this should be slightly lower than the dragon. This is the feminine side of the property. Ensure this area is kept clutter-free. Ideally plant a beautiful flowerbed or have an attractive garden feature here.

Other considerations

The ideal street placement is somewhere in the middle with equal tiger and dragon. Houses nearer one end or the other will have an imbalance of male and female energies in the home respective to whether there is more support for the dragon (male/yang) or the tiger (female/yin).

The perfect feng shui house will have all four animals present. Above all the symbol of the dragon should be present. Look for some hill or promontory that could be deemed to fulfil the role. The tiger is always present if the dragon is. They are the yin and yang of each other even if not visible to the eye.

If the land is flat on both sides, this is not necessarily bad feng shui. Often the celestial animals can be manifested through the design features of the house. For example, the chimney on the right-hand side of the house (as you look at it) will make the right side higher. Landscaping can create good feng shui, planting a tall vibrant tree, or several trees on the right-hand side of the house, will create the same dragon effect.

One last thing to be mindful of as a general tip – step back and cast your eye over the entire plot. Does its shape symbolically suggest anything detrimental – a ferocious animal, for example, or an aggressive arrow?

Applying feng shui to the process of buying a house is a wise investment. Good feng shui means positive energy, and everyone is naturally attracted to that, making your home easy to sell on when the time comes.

Location, location, location

From an estate agent's perspective this is always the master key that affects price. In feng shui terms it is also of vital importance and is about the quality of the chi entering the house. Look at the surroundings of your proposed house:

- Does the area look well maintained?

- What are the neighbours like?

- Check for sha chi from neighbouring structures, overwhelming buildings, power stations, pylons, radio masts, etc.

Ideally you want your new home to have space for you to grow and evolve. In classical feng shui it is considered auspicious to have more land at the back of the house than the front, especially if it is well contained within a strong boundary as this allows the energy of wealth to accumulate.

Generally water at the back of the house, especially if it is very close, is not ideal. Proportion is key; a healthy pond is fine while a huge fast-flowing river will rob the occupants of their beneficial chi. A body of water in front of the house, though, such as a fountain, lake, river or well-tended pond, is conversely excellent feng shui.

A house that overlooks or has a view of a cemetery is considered poor feng shui. A cemetery is a place of death, where the chi will be predominantly yin and slow-moving. Similarly a house beside or near a junkyard, used car lot or landfill site is best avoided as this type of mass clutter can be overwhelming and this degree of harmful chi is difficult to counteract.

Front door

Our vitally important mouth of chi, the front door, is the means whereby the house is either positively or detrimentally nourished. Often feng shui enthusiasts will calculate their personal best directions at this stage (Ming Gua Numbers) and find a house that sites the front door in one of their favourable directions. Whilst this is beneficial, it is not as vital as the general placement of the door. The stronger, healthier and more balanced the front door, the stronger and better the quality of chi available for those who live there. Make sure the front door is on the front of the house as side entrances can make it hard for the beneficial chi to find you.

A door that fits well with the size and proportion of the rest of the house and that opens widely without squeaking is ideal. Chi meanders and you need a winding path to your front door. Often a straight, direct path (aggressive chi) can be altered with landscaping but sometimes it just can't and such houses are best avoided, if possible. Similarly it is important that the name or number of the house is clearly visible and that the hardware and paintwork of the door and surrounding area looks well cared for – no cracked pots, dead flowers and overflowing rubbish bins. I appreciate these are things you can change once the house is purchased but an unkempt doorway will be indicative of the predecessor chi you are buying into and you may find you need to do more than paint the door once you move in! Avoid large, overpowering trees close to the front entrance, especially if they are less than healthy, they will block chi opportunities from finding you.

Check your new house doesn't have any of the major feng shui issues listed in Chapter 7 (*see page 131*). If it does, and you just 'know' this house is the one for you – can you solve them easily using one of the remedies suggested?

Environmental issues to avoid

Power stations generate massive energy, as do pylons, radio and telephone masts, substations, etc. The emanating chaos of energy can result in negative chi for the surrounding houses. If you have no choice, this is one instance where a powerful feng shui bagua mirror, placed outside, between you and the offending issue could be beneficial, as it will reflect negative chi away from your home. For this you would use the Early Heaven Sequence bagua (*see Chapter 3, page 56–57*) as this deflects back the image of perfection. You could also usefully plug in a Helios (*see the Resources section, page 228*) to harmonize the chi in your home.

Street layout

The layout of the street in relation to your home can carry either beneficial or negative chi to you. Cures for the following issues can be found in Chapter 7 (*see page 143*).

- Avoid a house on a street that forms a noose around it.

- Houses on busy roads and T-Junctions are subject to fast-moving, aggressive chi. People living in this situation will feel attacked by life and find it hard to hold on to beneficial opportunities.

- Dead-ends – if the house is at the end of the road it becomes the dumping ground for the chi, which will stagnate as there is no opportunity for it to continue its journey.

- Driveways should ideally end at your house and not run alongside your home and away through the garden or in another direction causing opportunities to bypass you.

Check the bagua of your prospective home

Whilst most feng shui issues can be remedied, if you have a choice then it is worth checking out the bagua of your prospective purchase to ascertain what's missing and what's not. Remember your home is a mirror of your life therefore it would be beneficial to have the wealth/ blessings (fourth house), relationships (second house) and career/life path (first house) all present. You will not always choose a home that is a perfect square or rectangle with all the houses of the bagua present. This isn't necessarily problematic and there are ways to solve these issues (*see Chapter 7, page 144*). Even if the house itself isn't a regular shape it helps if the plot of land it sits on is. The worst plots are triangular as these contain too much fire energy and sha chi and are hard to remedy successfully.

For similar reasons it would be best to avoid a house with a prominent bathroom in the centre. While you can install cures this placement can have a serious impact on your health and is not easy to counteract.

Exercise: Imagine living in your new home

If you have more than one choice of suitable new home then revisiting it from a distance in your mind's eye works brilliantly and can help you make up your mind. During the physical visit your mind is occupied with the estate agent and looking at the practical reality of the space. Meanwhile your unconscious mind is busy taking in everything else; all those subliminal feelings and sensations about whether this is a good space for you.

Sit quietly, close your eyes and revisit in your mind each of the houses you're considering in turn. Visualize walking up to the front door, entering the property, pausing, sensing the quality of the energy inside and then wandering freely around the space, noticing if you avoid any area, or any area feels uncomfortable or colder than the rest etc.

Imagine living there and what it feels like to do so. Before you bring the second house to mind, stand up, stretch and give yourself a little shake to clear the screen then do the same process with the next possibility.

Write down your experiences. This little exercise should have very quickly highlighted which house will be most beneficial for you. This is a good check exercise to do on any home you are considering moving into.

Selling your home with feng shui

Your home is probably your biggest asset and it makes sense to capitalize on your investment when selling it. Yet, we are, on the whole, so unaware of the impact our home has on others that a whole business called Home Staging has been created to deal with this issue of preparing houses for sale. Feng shui is a form of conscious home staging dealing with the intangible flow of the chi.

To sell your home fast, for the best market price, you need to ensure the energy is balanced and geared towards your ideal buyer. A buyer will buy what 'feels' right to them. If the feeling's right they'll overlook many other potential issues. Many things contribute to that 'feeling', both the unseen and the seen. You need to understand both to maximize the profits from your biggest asset.

In my experience buyers are less imaginative than you might think. They won't see that the junk room could be converted into a wonderful study or dining area, they will just see the junk. The art of home staging is to make it easy for your perfect buyers to picture themselves living in your home: cooking, playing with their children, relaxing, evolving. When the energy is unbalanced or there are energetic distractions, potential buyers might not know anything about feng shui, but they will feel the disharmony and won't make an offer.

First impressions do count

As we've discussed, the front door and entrance are THE most important areas of the house in feng shui. Ensure your entrance offers a warm and inviting welcome. This is the buyer's first impression and energetically conveys the condition of the rest of the house. Keep it immaculate. Trim back overhanging foliage around your doorway and the path leading up to it. Remove weeds, dead flowers, broken plant pots, children's abandoned toys and other eyesores.

Can buyers find you? Ensure your house name and number is clearly visible and preferably just above eye line; looking up creates an uplifting feeling whereas looking down creates the opposite. For the same reason if you have a double-digit house number the second number is best placed just above the first to create uplifting chi. Ensure the doorbell is working; so often I visit homes with notes on saying 'please knock loudly, bell not working' – this won't sell your house!

Make sure the entrance is well lit and have something flanking either side of the front door, such as two pots of lush, healthy plants and flowers. I don't particularly advocate decorating before selling, as buyers are likely to redo it to their tastes once they move in. But if your hallway is looking tired it is worth a fresh coat of paint here to give that sense of freshness when people enter. If you leave a raw onion, cut in half, overnight it will absorb the smell of fresh paint quickly and effectively.

Time to let go

Moving house is the ideal opportunity for a thorough clutter-clear. Think how much money you'll save in removal fees. More than that, you need to give potential buyers a feeling of space, and preferably a neutral space. Let go of all the things you've been holding onto – the things that are clogging up your life and keeping you stuck. Give yourself the best opportunity for a fresh start. Remember what you learnt in Chapter 5 (*see page 87*); start by picking up every item and asking yourself, 'Does it make my heart sing?'

If your cupboards are overstuffed and things are lying around with no home, buyers will get the feeling that this home is too small for your needs and therefore too small for theirs too.

Start packing up

I rarely suggest hiring storage units, as it's better to discard items rather than hide them. However, moving house is one such time when it can be beneficial so you can store personal items away from the prying eyes of prospective buyers. Some of your bulkier furniture could be stored away to create a sense of spaciousness in your home. Less is always more when it comes to preparing your home for sale.

From a feng shui perspective this symbolically creates space for another family to move in energetically and lets the universe know you are serious about moving out. Be careful not to take it to extremes though. I gave this advice to one client via email before I visited her space. When I did visit, every bookshelf and windowsill was empty and in the centre of each room were huge great packing crates filled with her belongings. We spent the afternoon retrieving a few choice items to make the space neutral and spacious yet homely and aspirational to a prospective buyer. It's all about balance.

Keep things neutral

Personal items such as family photographs or religious objects will distract potential buyers and are best packed away. You wouldn't want to buy a 'used' item as opposed to a new one nor do your buyers want to feel that way when purchasing their house; they want that sense of a 'new' home. Also if buyers are distracted by your collection of antique brasses or carriage clocks they won't be focusing on the selling points of your home and will have a harder time imagining the house as theirs rather than yours.

If things are broken or in bad condition buyers are likely to think your home hasn't been cared for and they may become concerned about bigger maintenance issues that have been neglected over the years. Fix what's obvious.

Exercise: Who's your perfect buyer?

Close your eyes and spend five minutes visualizing who you think your perfect buyer would be and what their style may be. Once you open your eyes look around your home and decide what needs to go or stay to attract that perfect buyer.

Symbolism is the language of the unconscious mind. Are you projecting the right image? Tweak symbolism towards aspirations of the perfect buyer. In other words, use symbolism to attract the person/people you want to buy the house. For example an executive home could use stunning landscape or portrait images of remote foreign places and people to create the energy of being well travelled and culturally aware.

Feng shui key

You only need one person, or one family, to fall in love with your home.

Engaging the senses

We are constantly responding positively or negatively to the subtle stimuli in our environment, whether it is our appetite stimulated by the smell of freshly baked bread or an instinctive move to turn away and cover our nose when some vehicle belches exhaust fumes at us. Engage the senses of your prospective buyers by ensuring that your home exudes the following qualities.

Feels good

Ensure the chi can move freely around your space; all passageways are clutter-free and nothing is stored behind doors preventing them from opening fully. Ensure there are no mirrors placed opposite doors or reflecting toilets. It's good to have some moving chi to keep the space stimulated – a ceiling fan, mobile or water feature placed near the front of the house. Keep the house at an even, ambient temperature. Avoid rough surfaces and sharp corners.

Looks good

Buyers respond to harmony. Enhance the sense of horizontal space in your home. This means clearing all surfaces, kitchen counters, shelves, dressers, etc. You want to draw the eye to the corner diagonal of each room, creating a sense of spaciousness. Once you've cleared the clutter, take a critical look at the state of your carpets and wall finishes – are they badly stained or scuffed? Could a few choice, inexpensive rugs or sheepskins solve the problem? Or perhaps you can rearrange the furniture to minimize the impact. Consider moving furniture in any event. It creates a more spacious room to have furniture placed away from the walls – the 'floating' arrangement we discussed in Chapter 8 (*see page 173*) – not great daily living feng shui but perfect for selling your home. Light up your space by keeping the lights on if necessary, especially in any dark corners.

Sounds good

Soft, non-intrusive background music (classical usually works best) will prevent your house from feeling 'dead' to buyers and helps create a sense of harmony. If the source of music is placed in the sixth house it will also activate the helpful friends/travel area, which is beneficial for sales. Eliminate noisy irritants such as dripping taps, washing machines, screaming children, barking dogs, lawn mowers, etc.

Smells good

More than any other sense, smell affects our emotional reaction. Our olfactory memory lives long. We all know the theory of freshly ground coffee and baking bread being the optimum signature scents for creating that welcoming homely feel. But a simple scented candle will work just as well to engage this sense. Basil, rosemary and vanilla are all good options but avoid anything too floral.

If you have pets it is best they are out of the house when showing people round; if they are non-pet lovers they can make negative judgements about the impact of pets on houses, and pets do often smell – get a trusted friend to do a smell test – not just pets, but old socks, mould, damp, smoke, chemicals, cooking odours, etc.

Advertising

Correctly place your 'for sale' sign to the right of the front door as you look at it. This is the yang, or dragon, side of the house. Draw a picture of a house on a small piece of paper, write SOLD across it and write the price you've sold it for. Place this under your front doormat. This has the effect of reminding the unconscious that the house is sold every time someone walks over the threshold.

Focus on the kitchen
This is the heart of your home so make this area gorgeous with clear counters and an organized pantry, and keep wastebaskets and knives out of sight. Pots of herbs and a bowl full of citrus fruit on the countertop add healthy zing.

Green fingers
Fresh flowers and healthy pot plants are a great way to enliven the chi and bring life to any space. Ensure there are no spindly plants climbing up the house (it makes the house seem like it's dying). Give all the plants in and around your house a good spruce up and replace anything that's wilting.

Insist that bathroom doors remain shut
Buyers should never see a toilet when they enter a house or a room. Toilet lids should remain down and doors to bathrooms should always be closed.

Exercise: Get a fresh perspective

Go outside your home and look at it as though you were the prospective buyer approaching. Better yet ask a friend to do this for you – it works best if your friend hasn't visited for a while. Write down all the thoughts and first impressions about your house that come to mind in the first 2–3 minutes. Don't censor the information. Selling your home is more about selling a feeling, rather than the actual bricks and mortar. Is there anything obvious you need to change?

Saying goodbye

Houses don't sell when occupants remain emotionally attached to them. I see this a lot in cases of divorce where one party is being forced to sell. It's not always possible to resolve these matters but do what you can to get everyone's consent. At the very least, remember the ethos of this book and honour the Spirit of Place that has nurtured, nourished and supported you for the time you have lived there. Walk around your home talking to it. Thank it for all the happy memories and tell it why you need to move on now and invite it to welcome in the new owners etc.

You can take this one step further by writing a letter to your home thanking it for looking after your family and sharing your willingness to let another family now benefit from it. Gather the family together and read it out loud to your house.

Feng shui tip

To help you let go. Take a small piece of the foundation of the property – maybe a stone or piece of brick from an unobtrusive corner, and throw it into a fast-moving stream or river and let the flow of the clean water carry you to your future.

My favourite way to leave one space and move to another is to stand in the centre of the space with arms outstretched and energetically gather up all the good times and memories the space holds, and then give yourself a hug, taking those happy energies inside. When you get to your new space stand in the centre of it and open your arms out wide, putting the happy chi into this new home. I did this with my husband as we left our marital home on getting divorced. It was a powerfully poignant moment and, yes, there were tears but it also reminded us of all the good times we had created in the space and enabled us both to take them with us into our new lives, and it meant the chi we left for the next occupants was as clean and clear as it could be.

If the house is being sold empty then make sure a trusted key holder visits to air the rooms regularly, to keep the garden tidy and perhaps use a scented room spray to freshen the environment – vanilla or lemongrass scents work best. This prevents stagnant chi accumulating and preventing a sale.

You've done everything and it still won't sell

When there's no obvious reason why a property hasn't been snapped up, there may be some less obvious ones, the two major ones being geopathic stress (GS) and predecessor chi. Estate agents refer to the latter as the three Ds: death, debt and divorce. If any of these are the reason for the property finding itself on the market then they are notoriously difficult to shift unless, of course, you space-clear them – if this applies to you follow the advice in Chapter 6 (*see page 113*). If you have geopathic stress follow the advice given in Chapter 10 or consider getting a professional consultant in to clear this for you.

Occasionally houses don't sell because they are attached to the wonderful care that has been taken of them by their current owners and the house is reluctant to let them go. In this instance tell the house you will find a good buyer who will care for the space just as well as you have. Engage the Spirit of Place in releasing you to your future.

If in doubt, always ask your home; it may sound strange, but by now you should have discovered your home is pretty chatty and will happily share its wisdom and maybe even some poignant 'home truths'. You may hear these messages in a number of different ways; you may suddenly get an inspiration to do something whilst doing the washing-up, or a friend makes a suggestion that is perfect, or you see the answer in a book, a magazine or on the TV. Stay open.

Exercise: Creating chi

The following is a wonderful way to create chi balance in your home, whenever you're feeling the need, whether buying, selling or just living.

For one week, place the four sacred elements in their cardinal directions in your home. These are the cardinal direction elements described in Chapter 2 (*see page 37 – not the five elements referred to on page 33*). You are the fifth element who will dance beautifully between them.

❖ **North** – A feather and a stick of incense to balance the air realm.

❖ **East** – A candle to balance the fire realm (never leave lit candles unattended – only light when at home).

❖ **South** – A crystal, rock or pot of earth to balance the earth realm.

❖ **West** – A shell or glass of water to balance the water realm.

FENG SHUI TIPS FOR BUYING AND SELLING YOUR HOME

- When buying a home always check the 'armchair' position; support at the back and sides, open at the front.

- Are the Land Spirits happy? Does the vegetation look healthy and vibrant?

- Check the history of the previous occupants. What story are you buying into?

- To sell your home make sure people can find you.

- Focus on creating a warm welcoming entrance.

- Clear the clutter, neutralize the space and let the chi flow.

- Energetically say goodbye and welcome the new owners in.

Conclusion

Chi Enters and Chi Leaves

'When you change the way you look at things, the things you look at change.'
WAYNE W. DYER

Your home is alive and listening to you. If you love and nurture your home it will love and nurture you in return. Nothing ever goes one way: the act of loving your home is effectively an act of self-love. If you come home and create a pleasant environment, do the five-minute tidy up, light some candles, add some ambient lighting and listen to some good music, you will enjoy the benefits of nourishing chi far more than if you come home and flop in front of the TV with a takeaway, surrounded by all the stuff you left on the floor that morning because you were in a hurry and there's nowhere for it to go anyway.

Feng shui works best in the utter simplicity of these small daily actions. A gorgeous vase of flowers makes the room look more attractive. A lush pot plant or a bowl of vibrant juicy, fresh fruit will immediately enliven the chi of a space, whereas a bowl of last night's stale washing-up will activate the detrimental chi. I encourage you to use your home to engage all your senses, explore symbolism, textures, colours and scents.

We are at the end of our journey together. I truly hope I have inspired you to change the relationship with your home and I would love to hear your stories of what worked for you. Feng shui won't solve every problem and guarantee you a carefree life until the day you die, but its practice will wake you up to the inherent magic that underlies all things. It will engage you in a deep personal journey of self-discovery and transformation. It will help you to manage your fear of change. It will give you a sense of empowerment and self-responsibility as you learn that you can affect change in your life simply by reorganizing your space and deeply connecting to your home. Say hello to your home when you walk in, give the walls or worktops a loving stroke. I encourage you to talk to your home – tell it your hopes and dreams, thank your home for supporting you and cocooning you safely. Regularly ask it what it needs from you – the answers may surprise you!

Enjoy creating a healing sanctuary for yourself. Take your time. Let it evolve as you evolve. Engage in this intimate relationship and before long you will have created a harmonious haven that becomes the healing hub from which you venture confidently out to conquer the world. Remember, no single feng shui solution lasts forever – what does last is the constantly changing dance between heaven and earth, between you and your environment, inviting the sheng chi and dispersing the sha chi.

Wishing you infinite health, wealth and happiness and a final reminder...

THE 10 COMMANDMENTS OF FENG SHUI

1. Clear the clutter.

2. Keep the front entrance of your home well maintained.

3. Allow chi to flow freely.

4. Contain the chi energy, i.e. don't let it rush by too quickly.

5. Make sure everything works.

6. Check out your home for negative earth energies.

7. Be aware of the images and symbols in your home.

8. Create a quiet sanctuary in your bedroom.

9. Make the kitchen a centre of calm.

10. Love your home and it will love you.

Resources

If you feel called to employ a consultant to assess your property professionally then I recommend you find a practitioner from the Feng Shui Society register of consultants at www.fengshuisociety.org.uk. The consultants practise a variety of feng shui approaches. But, by using the register, you will know that they are well trained in whatever feng shui they practise. I have been a member of the FSS for many years. If you feel called to the approach I take then you can book a consultation at www.davinamackail.com.

You can find more details of my work, consultations, workshops, talks and individual sessions on my website www.davinamackail.com. Please do email me with your feng shui stories of what worked for you – I'd love to hear from you.

For regular feng shui updates follow me on twitter @davinamackail

Space clearing

- Nitraj Incense and white sage smudge sticks can be purchased from www.davinamackail.com

Geopathic stress and EMFs

- If you want to learn more then the 'Radiofrequency, EMFs and Health Risks' article in the Powerwatch subscription section at www.powerwatch.org.uk has a detailed and up-to-date overview of the existing science on microwave frequency, EMFs and their effects on our health

- The Helios plug-in environment harmonizer can be purchased from www.davinamackail.com

- Dulwich Health is a good resource for further information on geopathic stress and sells Raditech machines, visit www.dulwichhealth.co.uk

- Orchid Dect low-radiation phones can be found at www.orchidgrp.com/j159

- For quartz phone shields see www.davinamackail.com

Recommended reading

- *Are You Sleeping in a Safe Place?* Rolf Gordon (Dulwich Health Society, 1989)

- *Geopathic Stress: How Earth Energies Affect Our Lives*, Jane Thurnell Read (Element Books, 1995)

- *How to Grow Fresh Air: 50 House Plants That Purify Your Home or Office,* B.C. Wolverton (Penguin Books, 1997)

Feng shui remedies

- Clear quartz and amethyst crystals can be found at www.davinamackail.com

- For frosted panels from your photographs for mirrored wardrobes, etc., contact Vahe Saboonchian at United Graphics (Unit 10 Wadsworth Business Centre, 21 Wadsworth Road, Perivale, Middlesex, UB6 7LQ; telephone 020 8997 6246; email: info@united-graphics.co.uk)

- For beautiful feng shui artwork see Carla Miles www.energeticart.co.uk

Dowsing and earth acupuncture

- You can purchase dowsing rods from www.davinamackail.com

- For more information on earth acupuncture training and for a list of professional dowsers see www.britishdowsers.org

- Moon calendar from www.infra-azure.com

ABOUT THE AUTHOR

Samjhana Moon

Davina MacKail, BA Hons, RGN, DFSNI, is an author, practising shaman and feng shui expert dedicated to empowering others to help themselves.

She discovered feng shui when working in Hong Kong and China in the early 1990s and holds a professional diploma in the Practise and Spirit of Feng Shui.

Besides running a busy practice for private and business clients, Davina teaches workshops and for many years ran the Advanced Feng Shui course for Channel 5's *House Doctor*, Anne Maurice. She is the 'healthy home' expert for a number of independent companies, and has featured in *Harper's Bazaar*, *Eve* magazine, *Good Housekeeping* and on ITV's *This Morning*.

www.davinamackail.com

HAY HOUSE

Look within

Join the conversation about latest products,
events, exclusive offers and more.

 Hay House UK

 @HayHouseUK

 @hayhouseuk

 healyourlife.com

We'd love to hear from you!